Workshop on Deep Learning Approaches for Low-Resource Natural Language Processing 2018

Held at ACL 2018

Melbourne, Australia
19 July 2018

ISBN: 978-1-5108-6721-5

ACL 2018

Deep Learning Approaches for Low-Resource Natural Language Processing (DeepLo)

Proceedings of the Workshop

July 19, 2018
Melbourne, Australia

Preface

The ACL 2018 Workshop on Deep Learning Approaches for Low-Resource Natural Language Porcessing took place on Thursday July 19, in Melbourne Australia, immediately following the main conference.

Natural Language Processing is being revolutionized by deep learning with neural networks. However, deep learning requires large amounts of annotated data, and its advantage over traditional statistical methods typically diminishes when such data is not available; for example, SMT continues to outperform NMT in many bilingually resource-poor scenarios. Large amounts of annotated data do not exist for many low-resource languages, and for high-resource languages it can be difficult to find linguistically annotated data of sufficient size and quality to allow neural methods to excel. Our workshop aimed to bring together researchers from the NLP and ML communities who work on learning with neural methods when there is not enough data for those methods to succeed out-of-the-box. Techniques of interest include self-training, paired training, distant supervision, semi-supervised and transfer learning, and human-in-the-loop algorithms such as active learning.

Our call for papers for this inaugural workshop met with a strong response. We received 22 paper submissions, of which 6 were "extended abstracts"—work that will be presented at the workshop, but will not appear in the proceedings in order to allow it to be published elsewhere. We accepted 10 papers and 5 extended abstracts. Our program covers a broad spectrum of applications and techniques. It was augmented by invited talks from Trevor Cohn (Melbourne), Sujith Ravi (Google), and Stefan Riezler (Heidelberg).

We would like to thank the members of the Program Committee for their timely and thoughtful reviews.

Reza Haffari, Colin Cherry, George Foster, Shahram Khadivi, and Bahar Salehi

Organizers:

Reza Haffari, Monash University
Colin Cherry, Google Research
George Foster, Google Research
Shahram Khadivi, eBay Research
Bahar Salehi, The University of Melbourne

Program Committee:

Isabelle Augenstein, University of Copenhagen
Mohit Bansal, The University of North Carolina
Daniel Beck, The University of Melbourne
Parminder Bhatia, Amazon
Colin Cherry, Google Research
Jacob Devlin, Google Research
Kevin Duh, Johns Hopkins University
Orhan Firat, Google Research
George Foster, Google Research
Reza Haffari, Monash University
Cong Vu Hoang, The University of Melbourne
Melvin Johnson, Google Research
Shahram Khadivi, eBay Research
Philipp Koehn, Johns Hopkins University
Julia Kreutzer, Heidelberg University
Gaurav Kumar, Johns Hopkins University
Patrick Littell, Carnegie Mellon University
Evgeny Matusov, eBay Research
David Mortensen, Carnegie Mellon University
Marek Rei, University of Cambridge
Sebastian Ruder, Insight Research Centre for Data Analytics
Bahar Salehi, The University of Melbourne
Nicola Ueffing, eBay Research

Invited Speakers:

Trevor Cohn, The University of Melbourne
Sujith Ravi, Google Research
Stefan Riezler, Heidelberg University

Table of Contents

Program

Thursday, July 19, 2018

9:00–9:10   *Opening Remarks*

9:10–9:50   *Invited Talk*
Stefan Riezler

9:50–10:30   *Invited Talk*
Sujith Ravi

10:30–11:00   **Coffee Break**

11:00–12:40   **Oral Presentations**

11:00–11:25   *Phrase-Based & Neural Unsupervised Machine Translation*
Guillaume Lample, Myle Ott, Alexis Conneau, Ludovic Denoyer and Marc'Aurelio Ranzato

11:25–11:50   *Character-level Supervision for Low-resource POS Tagging*
Katharina Kann, Johannes Bjerva, Isabelle Augenstein, Barbara Plank and Anders Søgaard

11:50–12:15   *Training a Neural Network in a Low-Resource Setting on Automatically Annotated Noisy Data*
Michael A. Hedderich and Dietrich Klakow

12:15–12:40   *Exploiting Cross-Lingual Subword Similarities in Low-Resource Document Classification*
Mozhi Zhang, Yoshinari Fujinuma and Jordan Boyd-Graber

12:40–14:00   **Lunch Break**

14:00–15:30   **Poster Session**

Multi-task learning for historical text normalization: Size matters
Marcel Bollmann, Anders Søgaard and Joachim Bingel

Compositional Language Modeling for Icon-Based Augmentative and Alternative Communication
Shiran Dudy and Steven Bedrick

Multimodal Neural Machine Translation for Low-resource Language Pairs using Synthetic Data
Koel Dutta Chowdhury, Mohammed Hasanuzzaman and Qun Liu

Morphological neighbors beat word2vec on the long tail
Clayton Greenberg, Mittul Singh and Dietrich Klakow

Multi-Task Active Learning for Neural Semantic Role Labeling on Low Resource Conversational Corpus
Fariz Ikhwantri, Samuel Louvan, Kemal Kurniawan, Bagas Abisena, Valdi Rachman, Alfan Farizki Wicaksono and Rahmad Mahendra

Domain Adapted Word Embeddings for Improved Sentiment Classification
Prathusha Kameswara Sarma, Yingyu Liang and Bill Sethares

Investigating Effective Parameters for Fine-tuning of Word Embeddings Using Only a Small Corpus
Kanako Komiya and Hiroyuki Shinnou

Dependency Parsing of Code-Switching Data with Cross-Lingual Feature Representations
KyungTae Lim, Niko Partanen, Michael Rießler and Thierry Poibeau

Semi-Supervised Learning with Auxiliary Evaluation Component for Large Scale e-Commerce Text Classification
Mingkuan Liu, Musen Wen, Selcuk Kopru, Xianjing Liu and Alan Lu

Low-rank passthrough neural networks
Antonio Valerio Miceli Barone

Embedding Transfer for Low-Resource Medical Named Entity Recognition: A Case Study on Patient Mobility
Denis Newman-Griffis and Ayah Zirikly

Character-level Supervision for Low-resource POS Tagging

Katharina Kann[1], Johannes Bjerva[2],
Isabelle Augenstein[2], Barbara Plank[3], Anders Søgaard[2]
[1]Center for Data Science, New York University, USA
[2]Department of Computer Science, University of Copenhagen, Denmark
[3]Department of Computer Science, IT University of Copenhagen, Denmark
kann@nyu.edu

Abstract

Neural part-of-speech (POS) taggers are known to not perform well with little training data. As a step towards overcoming this problem, we present an architecture for learning more robust neural POS taggers by jointly training a hierarchical, recurrent model and a recurrent character-based sequence-to-sequence network supervised using an auxiliary objective. This way, we introduce stronger character-level supervision into the model, which enables better generalization to unseen words and provides regularization, making our encoding less prone to overfitting. We experiment with three auxiliary tasks: lemmatization, character-based word autoencoding, and character-based random string autoencoding. Experiments with minimal amounts of labeled data on 34 languages show that our new architecture outperforms a single-task baseline and, surprisingly, that, on average, raw text autoencoding can be as beneficial for low-resource POS tagging as using lemma information. Our neural POS tagger closes the gap to a state-of-the-art POS tagger (MarMoT) for low-resource scenarios by 43%, even outperforming it on languages with templatic morphology, e.g., Arabic, Hebrew, and Turkish, by some margin.

1 Introduction

POS tagging, i.e., assigning syntactic categories to tokens in context, is an important first step when developing language technology for low-resource languages. POS tags can provide an efficient inductive bias for modeling downstream tasks, especially if training data for these tasks are limited.

However, POS tagging can be very challenging if only a few labeled sentences are available. Previous work on POS tagging with limited or no annotated data comes in three flavors, e.g., (Yarowsky et al., 2001; Goldwater and Griffiths, 2007; Li et al., 2012; Biemann, 2012; Täckström et al., 2013; Dong et al., 2015; Agić et al., 2015): unsupervised POS induction, cross-lingual transfer, or, if some suitable data are available, supervised induction from small labeled corpora or dictionaries. This work focuses on the latter: We explore the effect of multi-task learning for building robust POS taggers for low-resource languages from small amounts of annotated data.

In low-resource settings, neural POS taggers have been observed to perform poorly compared to log-linear models. This is unfortunate, since neural POS taggers have other advantages, including being easily integrable into multi-task learning architectures, sidestepping feature engineering, and providing compact word-level and sentence-level representations. In this paper, we therefore take steps to bridge the gap to state-of-the-art taggers in such scenarios.

Specifically, we consider training neural POS taggers from 478 annotated tokens (the size of the smallest treebank in UD 2.0[1]). In such a setting, it is often useful to leverage data from other, related tasks (Bingel and Søgaard, 2017), if available. However, since for many low-resource languages such data is hard to find, we consider multi-task learning scenarios with no other sequence labeling data at hand:

(i) a scenario in which type-based morphological information is available, e.g., word-lemma pairs as can be found in standard dictionaries or UniMorph,[2]

---

[1]http://universaldependencies.org/
[2]http://unimorph.org/

1

Proceedings of the Workshop on Deep Learning Approaches for Low-Resource NLP, pages 1–11
Melbourne, Australia July 19, 2018. ©2018 Association for Computational Linguistics

(ii) a scenario where we only rely on raw text corpora in the language, and

(iii) a scenario where we do not assume any additional data, but construct a synthetic auxiliary task instead.

In order to include secondary information such as word-lemma pairs into our model, we integrate a character-based recurrent sequence-to-sequence model into a hierarchical long short-term memory (LSTM) sequence tagger (cf. Figure 1). By formulating suitable auxiliary tasks (lemmatization, word autoencoding or random string autoencoding, respectively), we can include additional character-level supervision into our model via multi-task training.

Contributions. We present a novel architecture for inducing more robust neural POS taggers from small samples of annotated data in low-resource languages, combining a hierarchical, deep bi LSTM sequence tagger with a character-based sequence-to-sequence model. Furthermore, we experiment with different choices of external resources and corresponding auxiliary tasks and show that autoencoding can be as efficient as an auxiliary task for low-resource POS tagging as lemmatization. Finally, we evaluate our models on 34 typologically diverse languages.

2   POS Tagging with Subword-level Supervision

Hierarchical POS tagging LSTMs that receive both word-level and subword-level input, such as Plank et al. (2016), are known to perform well on unseen words. This is due to their ability to associate subword-level patterns with POS tags. However, hierarchical LSTMs are also very expressive, and thus prone to overfitting. We believe that using subword-level auxiliary tasks to regularize the character-level encoding in hierarchical LSTMs is a flexible and efficient way to get the best of both worlds: such a model is still able to make predictions about unknown words, but the subword-level auxiliary task should prevent it from overfitting.

2.1   Hierarchical LSTMs with Character-level Decoding

Our proposed multi-task architecture is shown in Figure 1. For the hierarchical sequence labeling LSTM, we follow Plank et al. (2016): Our

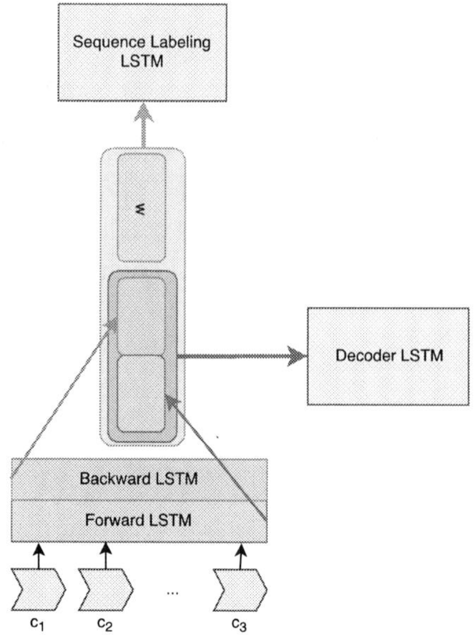

Figure 1: Our multi-task architecture, consisting of a shared character LSTM (down), as well as a sequence labeling (up) and a sequence-to-sequence (right) part.

subword-level LSTM is bi-directional and operates on the character level (Ling et al., 2015; Ballesteros et al., 2015). Its input is the character sequence of each input word, represented by the embedding sequence $c_1, c_2, \ldots, c_m$. The final character-based representation of each word is the concatenation of the two last LSTM hidden states:

$$v_{c,i} = conc(\text{LSTM}_{c,f}(c_{1:m}), \qquad (1)$$
$$\text{LSTM}_{c,b}(c_{m:1}))$$

Second, a context bi-LSTM operates on the word level. Like Plank et al. (2016), we use the term "context bi-LSTM" to denote a bidirectional LSTM which, in order to generate a representation for input element i, encodes all elements up to position i with a forward LSTM and all elements from n to i using a backward LSTM. For each sentence represented by embeddings $w_1, w_2, \ldots, w_n$, its input are the concatenation of the word embeddings with the outputs of the subword-level LSTM: $conc(w_1, v_{c,1}), conc(w_2, v_{c,2}) \ldots, conc(w_n, v_{c,n})$. The final representation which gets forwarded to the next part of the network is again the concatenation of the last two hidden LSTM states:

$$v_{w,i} = conc(\text{LSTM}_{w,f}(conc(w, v_c)_{1:i}), \quad (2)$$
$$\text{LSTM}_{w,b}(conc(w, v_c)_{n:i}))$$

This is then passed on to a classification layer.

2.1.1 Character-based Decoding

We extend the network with a new component, a character-based sequence-to-sequence model. It consists of a bidirectional LSTM encoder which is connected to an LSTM decoder (Cho et al., 2014; Sutskever et al., 2014).

Encoding. The encoder corresponds to the character-level bi-directional LSTM described above and thus yields the representation

$$v_{c,i} = conc(\text{LSTM}_{c,f}(c_{1:m}), \quad (3)$$
$$\text{LSTM}_{c,b}(c_{m:1}))$$

for an input word embedded as $c_1, c_2, \ldots, c_m$. Parameters of the character-level LSTM are shared between the sequence labeling and the sequence-to-sequence part of our model.

Decoding. The decoder receives the concatenation of the last hidden states $v_{c,i}$ as input. In particular, we do not use an attention mechanism (Bahdanau et al., 2015), since our goal is not to improve performance on the auxiliary task, but instead to encourage the encoder to learn better word representations. The decoder is trained to predict each output character y_t dependent on $v_{c,i}$ and previous predictions $y_1, \ldots, y_{t-1}$ as

$$p(y_t|\{y_1, \ldots, y_{t-1}\}, v_{c,i}) = g(y_{t-1}, s_t, v_{c,i}) \quad (4)$$

for a non-linear function g and the LSTM hidden state s_t. The final softmax output layer is calculated over the vocabulary of the language.

Joint model. Figure 1 shows how parameters are shared between the sequence labeling and the sequence-to-sequence components of our network. All model parameters, including all embeddings, are updated during training. Our model architecture is "symmetric", i.e., it does not distinguish between main and auxiliary tasks. However, we use early stopping on the development set of the main task, such that convergence is not guaranteed for the auxiliary tasks.

2.2 Multi-task Learning

We want to train our neural model jointly on (i) a low-resource main task, i.e., POS tagging, and (ii) an exchangeable auxiliary task (cf. §3). Therefore, we want to maximize the following joint log-likelihood:

$$\mathcal{L}(\boldsymbol{\theta}) = \sum_{(l,s) \in \mathcal{D}_{POS}} \log p_\theta\,(l \mid s) \quad (5)$$
$$+ \sum_{(in,out) \in \mathcal{D}_{aux}} \log p_\theta\,(out \mid in)$$

Here, $\mathcal{D}_{POS}$ denotes the POS tagging training data, with s being the input sentence and l the corresponding label sequence. $\mathcal{D}_{aux}$ is a placeholder for our auxiliary task training data with examples consisting of input in and output out. We experiment with three different auxiliary tasks, which will be described in the next section.

The set of model parameters $\boldsymbol{\theta}$ is the union of the set of parameters of the sequence labeling and the sequence-to-sequence part. Parameters of the character LSTM are shared between the main and the auxiliary task.

3 (Un)supervised Auxiliary Tasks

In this section, we will describe our three auxiliary tasks in more detail.

3.1 Random String Autoencoding

Random string autoencoding is a synthetic auxiliary task created for a setting in which we have no additional resources available. It consists of, given a random character sequence as input, reconstructing the same sequence in the output. Concretely, given the alphabet $\mathcal{A}_L$ of a language L, the task is to learn a mapping $r \mapsto r$ for $r \in \mathcal{A}_L^+$. Note that the random string r is in most cases not a valid word in L. Additionally, we prepend a special symbol $\mathcal{S}_r$ to the input which indicates the current task to the encoder, e.g., "OUT=AE" or "OUT=POS".

3.2 Word Autoencoding

Word autoencoding is a special case of the previous auxiliary task, in that we now use actual words in the language, e.g., from unlabeled corpora or dictionaries. As for random string autoencoding, the task consists of reproducing a given input character sequence in the output. As before, we additionally feed a special symbol $\mathcal{S}_w$ into the model which signals the current task to the encoder. Our final training examples are of the form $(S_w; w) \mapsto w$, where $w \in V_L$ for the vocabulary V_L of L. Word autoencoding has been used as an auxiliary task before, e.g., (Vosoughi et al., 2016).

3.3 Lemmatization

Lemmatization is a task from the area of inflectional morphology. In particular, it is a special case of morphological inflection. Its goal is to map a given inflected word form to its lemma, e.g.,

$$\text{sueño} \mapsto \text{soñar}. \tag{6}$$

Sequence-to-sequence models have shown strong performances on morphological inflection (Aharoni et al., 2016; Kann and Schütze, 2016; Makarov et al., 2017). Therefore, when morphological dictionaries are available, we can easily combine a neural model for lemmatization with a POS tagger, using our architecture. Our intuition for this auxiliary task is that it should be possible to include morphological information into our character-based word representations.

Formally, the task can be described as follows. Let $\mathcal{A}_L$ be a discrete alphabet for language L and let $\mathcal{T}_L$ be a set of morphological tags for L. The morphological paradigm π of a lemma w in L is a set of pairs

$$\pi(w) = \left\{ \left(f_k[w], t_k \right) \right\}_{k \in T(w)} \tag{7}$$

where $f_k[w_\ell] \in \mathcal{A}_L^+$ is an inflected form, $t_k \in \mathcal{T}_L$ is its morphological tag and $T(w)$ is the respective set of paradigm slots. Lemmatization consists of predicting the lemma w for an inflected form $f_k[w_\ell]$ in $\pi(w)$.

4 Experimental Setup

In this section, we will describe our experiments, including data, baselines, and hyperparameters.

4.1 Data

POS. The data for our POS tagging main task comes from the Universal Dependencies (*UD*) 2.0 collection (Nivre et al., 2007). We use the provided train/dev/test splits.

Since we use the official datasets from the SIGMORPHON 2017 shared task on universal morphological reinflection (Cotterell et al., 2017) for the lemmatization auxiliary task, we limit ourselves to the languages featured there. We simulate a low-resource setting by reducing all training

sets to 478 tokens. Among our languages, this is the size of the smallest training set in UD 2.0.

Lemmatization. For the lemmatization auxiliary task, we make use of the word-lemma pairs in the training sets released for the SIGMORPHON 2017 shared task (Cotterell et al., 2017), which are subsets of the UniMorph data. In particular, there are three settings with different training sets per language: low (100 examples), medium (1,000 examples) and high (10,000 examples).

Word autoencoding. For the word autoencoding task, we use the inflected forms from the SIGMORPHON 2017 shared task dataset for each respective setting. Due to identical forms for different slot in the morphological paradigm of some lemmas, we might have duplicate examples in those datasets.

Random string autoencoding. For the random string autoencoding auxiliary task, we generate random character sequences to be used as training instances for our model's encoder-decoder part. In order to have the same amount of unique characters as with the other two auxiliary tasks, we use the character sets from the SIGMORPHON shared task vocabulary for each respective setting. We then uniformly draw characters from these sets and form strings of random lengths between 3 and 20 characters.

4.2 Baselines

TreeTagger. Since low-resource settings like the one considered here are known to be challenging for neural models, we employ TreeTagger (Schmid, 1995), a non-neural Markov model tagger, as our first baseline.

MarMoT. Our second non-neural baseline is the state-of-the-art tagger MarMoT (Müller et al., 2013), which is based on conditional random fields (CRFs, Lafferty et al. (2001)).

Single-task hierarchical LSTM. We compare all our results to a single-task baseline model, which corresponds largely to the architecture used by Plank et al. (2016) for POS tagging. We modify their original code by adding character dropout with a coefficient of 0.25 to improve regularization and make the baseline more comparable to and competitive with our models.

Multi-task baseline. We further compare to a multi-task architecture which jointly learns to predict the POS tag and the log-frequency of a word as suggested by Plank et al. (2016). The intuition described by the original authors is that the auxiliary loss, being predictive of word frequency, can improve the representations of rare words. Note that this baseline can easily be combined with our architecture. We leave the exploration of such a combination for future work.

4.3 Hyperparameters

For all networks, we use 300-dimensional character embeddings, 64-dimensional word embeddings and 100-dimensional LSTM hidden states. Encoder and decoder LSTMs have 1 hidden layer each. For training, we use ADAM (Kingma and Ba, 2014), as well as word dropout and character dropout, each with a coefficient of 0.25 (Kiperwasser and Goldberg, 2016). Gaussian noise is added to the concatenation of the last states of the character LSTMs for POS tagging. All models are trained using early stopping, with a minimum number of 75 (single-task and low), 30 (medium) or 20 (high) epochs and a maximum number of 300 epochs, which is never reached. We stop training if we obtain no improvement for 10 consecutive epochs. The best model on the development set is used for testing.

5   Results

The test results for all languages and settings are presented in Table 1.

Our first observation is that using 100 words of auxiliary task data seems to be sufficient, as we do not see consistent gains from adding more auxiliary task instances. This might be related to the very limited amount of POS tagging data we assume available; a too low main-auxiliary task data ratio probably inhibits further gains.

Second, we find that lemmatization and word autoencoding on average over all languages bring similar gains, differences are only between 0.0013 (medium) and 0.0021 (high) absolute accuracy. Comparing word and random string autoencoding, two observations can be made: in the low setting, differences are small, while random string autoencoding is the only task which performs worse in the high compared to the low setting. So the gap between the two autoencoding tasks grows bigger for larger auxiliary task data. This might be

explained by random string autoencoding being helpful in order to get clearer distinctions between characters; however, this might as well destroy the model's ability to pick up on beneficial similarities.

Our third observation is that lemmatization and word autoencoding consistently outperform the auxiliary task of predicting log-frequencies as suggested in Plank et al. (2016) with up to 0.0081 (POS+AE, low/high) higher absolute accuracy; random string autoencoding performs 0.0079 better in the low setting. We may thus conclude that, in our setting, auxiliary tasks with additional character-level supervision are more beneficial.

Fourth, both non-neural baselines outperform the single-task neural model. Adding auxiliary tasks leads to a higher performance (averaged over languages) than TreeTagger. MarMoT is the overall best performing model. However, for some individual languages, the neural model obtains higher accuracies, e.g., for Bulgarian, Dutch, or Romanian. In particular, our approach is stronger for languages with templatic morphology, e.g., Arabic, Hebrew, or Turkish. This emphasizes the importance of neural approaches for the task.

Finally, we look at differences between auxiliary tasks for individual languages. Here, we notice that autoencoders often outperform lemmatization for agglutinative languages. An explanation for this might be that agglutinative morphology is harder to learn, and the chance of overfitting on a small sample is therefore higher.

6   Analysis

6.1   Error Analysis

Table 2 lists the F_1-scores of our models across POS tags, compared to the single-task baseline.

Our first observation is that the decrease in performance from training on *more* random strings, is relatively equal across tags, with the exception of DET, PUNCT and X; tokens that consist of very few, fixed characters. We also note that all our models with character-level supervision get worse at predicting numerals. In contrast, ADP, AUX, CCONJ and PUNCT always benefit from a character-based auxiliary task. Generally, the POS taggers trained on small amounts of data are challenged by rare syntactic categories such as interjections and the miscellaneous category X.

language	high			medium			low			baselines			
	POS+ Lemma	POS+ AE	POS+ AE-Random	POS+ Lemma	POS+ AE	POS+ AE-Random	POS+ Lemma	POS+ AE	POS+ AE-Random	POS+ LogFrequ	POS	TreeTagger	MarMoT
arabic	**.6900(.01)**	.6862(.01)	.6747(.01)	.6638(.02)	.6737(.01)	.6635(.00)	.6735(.01)	.6680(.01)	.6731(.01)	.6583(.02)	.6545(.01)	.6047(.00)	.6398(.00)
basque	.5925(.01)	.6231(.01)	.5866(.01)	.6088(.01)	.6291(.01)	.6170(.01)	.6332(.01)	.6262(.01)	.6363(.00)	.6058(.01)	.6217(.02)	.6143(.00)	**.6862(.00)**
bulgarian	.6139(.01)	.6344(.01)	.5954(.01)	.6239(.01)	.6343(.00)	.6153(.02)	.6267(.01)	.6410(.01)	**.6431(.01)**	**.6431(.01)**	.6272(.01)	.6208(.00)	.6067(.00)
catalan	.7104(.01)	.7139(.01)	.7051(.00)	.7175(.01)	.7212(.01)	.7116(.01)	.7279(.01)	.7352(.01)	.7232(.01)	.7024(.01)	.7197(.01)	.7525(.00)	**.7824(.00)**
czech	.6227(.01)	.6063(.01)	.5574(.02)	.5923(.01)	.5953(.00)	.5742(.01)	.6131(.02)	.6048(.00)	.6003(.01)	.5784(.01)	.5897(.02)	.6417(.00)	**.6720(.00)**
danish	.6368(.00)	.6322(.01)	.6137(.01)	.6431(.01)	.6434(.00)	.6307(.01)	.6375(.01)	.6378(.00)	.6378(.00)	.6431(.01)	.6346(.03)	.6346(.00)	**.6703(.00)**
dutch	**.5901(.01)**	.5835(.01)	.5533(.01)	.5837(.00)	.5778(.00)	.5689(.01)	.5810(.01)	.5807(.00)	.5812(.01)	.5559(.01)	.5724(.01)	.5406(.00)	.5866(.00)
english	.5784(.01)	.5723(.01)	.5183(.01)	.5747(.01)	.5658(.01)	.5423(.00)	.5585(.03)	.5836(.01)	.5857(.00)	.5751(.02)	.5822(.02)	.6019(.00)	**.6507(.00)**
estonian	.5386(.01)	.5456(.01)	.5224(.01)	.5438(.01)	.5323(.01)	.5173(.01)	.5384(.01)	.5474(.01)	.5333(.02)	.5388(.01)	.5391(.02)	.5632(.00)	**.5851(.00)**
finnish	**.5748(.01)**	.5678(.01)	.5403(.02)	.5599(.01)	.5632(.01)	.5468(.01)	.5637(.01)	.5616(.01)	.5634(.00)	.5424(.01)	.5525(.01)	.5602(.00)	.5743(.00)
french	.6922(.01)	.6898(.01)	.6720(.00)	.6855(.01)	.6874(.00)	.6876(.01)	.7048(.00)	.6981(.00)	.6924(.01)	.6858(.01)	.6826(.01)	.5931(.00)	**.7084(.00)**
german	.6804(.01)	.6742(.00)	.5739(.02)	.6887(.00)	.6639(.01)	.6190(.01)	.6768(.01)	.6830(.01)	.6687(.01)	.6895(.01)	.6711(.01)	.5912(.00)	**.7370(.00)**
hebrew	.6764(.00)	**.6838(.00)**	.6827(.01)	.6734(.01)	.6781(.00)	.6672(.00)	.6761(.01)	.6825(.00)	.6796(.01)	.6776(.01)	.6655(.01)	.6147(.00)	.6705(.00)
hindi	.5954(.01)	**.6062(.01)**	.5874(.01)	.5914(.01)	.5984(.01)	.5839(.01)	.5989(.01)	.6046(.01)	.6001(.01)	.5992(.01)	.5791(.02)	.5784(.00)	.5943(.00)
hungarian	.5820(.01)	.5853(.01)	.5647(.01)	.5811(.01)	.5836(.01)	.5712(.01)	.5907(.01)	.5897(.01)	.5991(.00)	.5824(.01)	.5825(.02)	.6352(.00)	**.6651(.00)**
irish	**.6800(.01)**	.6715(.01)	.6573(.00)	.6741(.00)	.6649(.00)	.6593(.01)	.6735(.00)	.6743(.00)	.6790(.00)	.6724(.01)	.6699(.00)	.6511(.00)	.6729(.00)
italian	.7150(.00)	.7123(.01)	.6992(.00)	.7105(.00)	.7032(.00)	.7012(.00)	.7012(.01)	.7054(.01)	.7053(.00)	.7076(.01)	.6902(.02)	.6959(.00)	**.7280(.00)**
latin	.5950(.00)	.5853(.01)	.5633(.01)	.6026(.01)	.5953(.00)	.5863(.00)	.5998(.01)	.6068(.01)	.5992(.01)	.6069(.00)	.6046(.01)	.6234(.00)	**.6312(.00)**
latvian	.5446(.01)	.5557(.01)	.5288(.01)	.5406(.01)	.5453(.01)	.5303(.01)	.5344(.01)	.5356(.01)	.5408(.01)	.5382(.00)	.5300(.01)	**.5984(.00)**	.5773(.00)
lithuanian	.5347(.01)	.5292(.02)	.4936(.01)	.5123(.01)	.5192(.01)	.5213(.01)	.5230(.01)	.5313(.01)	.5327(.01)	.5238(.01)	.4721(.01)	.5783(.00)	**.5840(.00)**
n.-bokmaal	.5388(.00)	.5399(.01)	.5048(.01)	.5352(.01)	.5368(.01)	.5280(.01)	.5365(.01)	.5400(.01)	.5437(.01)	.5300(.01)	.5016(.02)	**.5737(.00)**	.5658(.00)
n.-nynorsk	.6172(.01)	.6223(.01)	.6043(.01)	.6200(.01)	.6228(.01)	.6167(.01)	.6256(.01)	**.6263(.01)**	.6232(.01)	.6238(.01)	.6130(.01)	.6142(.00)	.6168(.00)
persian	.7419(.01)	.7438(.01)	.7287(.01)	.7312(.01)	.7277(.01)	.7330(.00)	.7332(.00)	.7352(.00)	.7340(.00)	.7278(.01)	.7116(.01)	.7339(.00)	**.7539(.00)**
polish	.6407(.00)	.6423(.01)	.5960(.01)	.6314(.01)	.6243(.01)	.6162(.01)	.6448(.00)	.6460(.01)	.6400(.01)	.6243(.01)	.6489(.01)	**.6712(.00)**	.6700(.00)
portuguese	.6886(.00)	.6865(.00)	.6597(.01)	.6786(.01)	.6775(.01)	.6692(.01)	.6784(.00)	.6815(.00)	.6920(.01)	.6482(.03)	.6408(.02)	.6377(.00)	**.7135(.00)**
romanian	.6029(.01)	**.6156(.01)**	.5956(.01)	.6028(.01)	.6117(.01)	.5969(.00)	.6027(.01)	.6135(.01)	.6145(.01)	.6062(.01)	.6051(.00)	.5993(.00)	.5740(.00)
russian	.6807(.01)	.6817(.01)	.6283(.00)	.6860(.02)	.6607(.01)	.6504(.01)	.6752(.01)	.6661(.01)	.6661(.01)	.6644(.01)	.6241(.05)	.6105(.00)	**.7281(.00)**
slovak	.6169(.01)	.6327(.01)	.5835(.01)	.6274(.01)	.6203(.01)	.6337(.02)	.6585(.01)	.6378(.01)	.6443(.01)	.6536(.02)	.6264(.02)	.6642(.00)	**.6672(.00)**
slovene	.6364(.00)	.6414(.00)	.6093(.01)	.6343(.01)	.6223(.01)	.6070(.01)	.6358(.00)	.6375(.01)	.6350(.01)	.6105(.01)	.5922(.02)	**.6561(.00)**	.6046(.00)
spanish	.6962(.00)	.6891(.01)	.6624(.02)	.6844(.01)	.6797(.01)	.6659(.01)	.6818(.01)	.6939(.01)	.6900(.01)	.6917(.01)	.6724(.01)	.6933(.00)	**.7578(.00)**
swedish	.6127(.01)	.6261(.01)	.5909(.01)	.6254(.00)	.6262(.00)	.6194(.01)	.6193(.01)	.6254(.01)	.6254(.00)	.6274(.01)	.6117(.02)	.6290(.00)	**.6304(.00)**
turkish	.6067(.01)	.6007(.01)	.5725(.01)	.5846(.01)	.5879(.00)	.5792(.01)	.6042(.01)	.6003(.01)	.6040(.01)	.6087(.01)	.5891(.01)	**.6107(.00)**	.6025(.00)
ukrainian	.5910(.01)	.5946(.00)	.5755(.00)	.5826(.01)	.5750(.00)	.5668(.01)	.5878(.02)	.5895(.01)	.5894(.01)	.5869(.02)	.5932(.01)	.5297(.00)	**.6125(.00)**
urdu	.6589(.01)	.6697(.01)	.6335(.00)	.6572(.01)	.6599(.00)	.6465(.01)	.6578(.01)	.6526(.01)	.6600(.01)	.6395(.02)	.6096(.03)	.5229(.00)	**.6776(.00)**
average	.6286(-)	.6307(-)	.6010(-)	.6251(-)	.6238(-)	.6131(-)	.6287(-)	.6307(-)	.6305(-)	.6226(-)	.6141(-)	.6188(-)	**.6529(-)**

Table 1: Averaged accuracies and standard deviations over 5 training runs on UD 2.0 test sets, with 478 tokens of POS-annotated data and varying amounts of data for the auxiliary task (low, medium and high). Best result for each language in bold. Autoencoding and lemmatization are *on par* across the board, and with 100 training sentences (low), random autoencoding is also competitive.

6.2 Why does Random String Autoencoding Help?

In the low setting, i.e., when using only 100 auxiliary task examples, autoencoding, especially of random strings, works better than or equally well as lemmatization for highly agglutinative languages such as Basque, Finnish, Hungarian, and Turkish. Further, while random string autoencoding is in general less efficient than autoencoding or lemmatization, it performs on par with these auxiliary tasks in the set-up with least auxiliary task data. However, this raises the question why random string autoencoding does work at all for a POS tagging main task. We offer two potential explanations:

General properties of the auxiliary tasks. Bingel and Søgaard (2017) showed that multi-task learning is more likely to be helpful when the auxiliary loss does not plateau earlier than the main loss. Figure 2 presents the loss curves for one model for each of four randomly selected languages (the corresponding plots for the remaining languages look similar). They show exactly the patterns found to be predictive of multi-task learning gains by Bingel and Søgaard (2017), who offer the explanation that when the auxiliary loss does not plateau before the target task, it can help the model out of local minima during training.

Preventing character collisions. A random string autoencoder needs to memorize the input string. This means encoding which characters are at what position in the input sequence. Jointly learning a random string autoencoder thus forces a model to make it easy to differentiate between characters, pushing them apart in vector space. See Table 3 for the average character distances and Table 4 for the minimum character distances across languages for our three systems (low setting) and our single-task baseline. For each system, the score is obtained by first calculating the average distance between all characters or, respectively, finding the minimum distance between any two characters for each language, and then computing the average across all languages.

Tag	high			medium			low			POS
	Δ Lemma	Δ AE	Δ AE-Rand.	Δ Lemma	Δ AE	Δ AE-Rand.	Δ Lemma	Δ AE	Δ AE-Rand.	
ADJ	-0.0090	0.0083	-0.0555	-0.0167	-0.0017	-0.0290	0.0139	0.0145	0.0045	0.4756
ADP	0.0308	0.0288	0.0042	0.0440	0.0345	0.0205	0.0356	0.0313	0.0293	0.7687
ADV	-0.0008	-0.0133	-0.0426	-0.0180	-0.0108	-0.0233	0.0166	0.0209	0.0193	0.2958
AUX	0.0610	0.0537	0.0203	0.0479	0.0264	0.0102	0.0250	0.0423	0.0300	0.6172
CCONJ	0.0849	0.0511	0.0400	0.0579	0.0449	0.0512	0.0646	0.0560	0.0606	0.7594
CONJ	0.0230	-0.0588	-0.0316	-0.0342	0.0674	0.1477	-0.0128	-0.1287	-0.0294	0.6617
DET	0.0227	0.0234	0.0048	0.0178	0.0210	-0.0151	0.0063	0.0046	-0.0037	0.6938
INTJ	-0.0204	-0.0072	-0.0022	-0.0229	-0.0133	-0.0086	-0.0217	-0.0115	-0.0166	0.0806
NOUN	0.0015	0.0127	-0.0226	-0.0009	0.0072	-0.0055	0.0099	0.0147	0.0076	0.5457
NUM	-0.0537	-0.0777	-0.1332	-0.1389	-0.1626	-0.1372	-0.0830	-0.0633	-0.0885	0.5965
PART	0.0313	0.0195	-0.0252	0.0089	-0.0280	-0.0558	-0.0221	-0.0046	-0.0013	0.6719
PRON	0.0532	0.0389	-0.0084	0.0435	0.0297	-0.0059	0.0346	0.0391	0.0368	0.5189
PROPN	-0.0374	-0.0529	-0.1133	-0.0682	-0.0503	-0.0684	-0.0318	-0.0197	-0.0249	0.4271
PUNCT	0.0342	0.0204	0.0192	0.0188	0.0187	0.0186	0.0199	0.0185	0.0142	0.9299
SCONJ	0.0243	0.0346	0.0000	0.0288	0.0116	-0.0073	0.0205	0.0102	0.0166	0.5708
SYM	-0.0495	-0.1380	-0.0482	-0.0590	0.0394	0.0072	0.1261	0.1738	0.1496	0.6437
VERB	0.0334	0.0397	-0.0268	0.0314	0.0234	0.0000	0.0416	0.0224	0.0378	0.4370
X	0.0829	0.0754	0.0262	0.0194	0.0175	0.0092	0.0126	0.0023	0.0019	0.1322

Table 2: F-score deltas between the neural single-task baseline (POS) and our multi-task systems.

System	Average Distance		
	low	medium	high
POS+Lemmatization	0.928	0.976	0.964
POS+AE	0.923	0.965	0.960
POS+AE-Random	0.913	0.956	0.996
POS		0.881	

Table 3: Average character embedding distances, averaged over all languages.

System	Minimum Distance		
	low	medium	high
POS+Lemmatization	0.031	0.027	0.074
POS+AE	0.032	0.031	0.092
POS+AE-Random	0.033	0.032	0.104
POS		0.018	

Table 4: Minimum character embedding distances, averaged over all languages.

In small sample regimes, pushing individual characters further apart is a potential advantage, since character collisions can be hurtful at inference time. We note how this is analogous to feature swamping of covariate features, as described in Sutton et al. (2006). Sutton et al. (2006) use a group lasso regularizer to prevent feature swamping. In the same way, we could also detect distributionally similar characters and use a group lasso regularizer to prevent covariate characters to swamp each other. However, this effect can potentially also hurt performance if done in an uninformed way. We intuit that this makes it also impossible for the model to learn useful similarities between characters (random string autoencoding in the high setting has a minimum distance of 0.104 compared to 0.018 for the single-task model). This might explain the performance gap between random string encoding and the other two auxiliary tasks for the high setting.

7 Related Work

POS tagging. POS tagging and other NLP sequence labeling tasks have been successfully approached using bidirectional LSTMs (Wang et al., 2015; Plank et al., 2016; Yang et al., 2016). Although previous work using such architectures often relies on massive datasets, Plank et al. (2016) show that bi-LSTMs in particular are not as reliant on large amounts of data in a sequence labeling scenario as previously assumed. Furthermore, their model is also a multi-task model, being trained jointly on predicting the POS and the log-frequency of a word. Their architecture obtained state-of-the-art results for POS tagging in several languages. Hence, in the low-resource setting considered here, we build upon the architecture developed by Plank et al. (2016), and extend it to a multi-task architecture involving sequence-to-sequence learning. Note though that in contrast to our setup, their tasks are both sequence-labeling tasks and using the same input for both tasks.

The same holds true for the multi-task model by Rei (2017), which is used to investigate how an additional language modeling objective could improve performance for sequence labeling without any need for additional training data. He reported

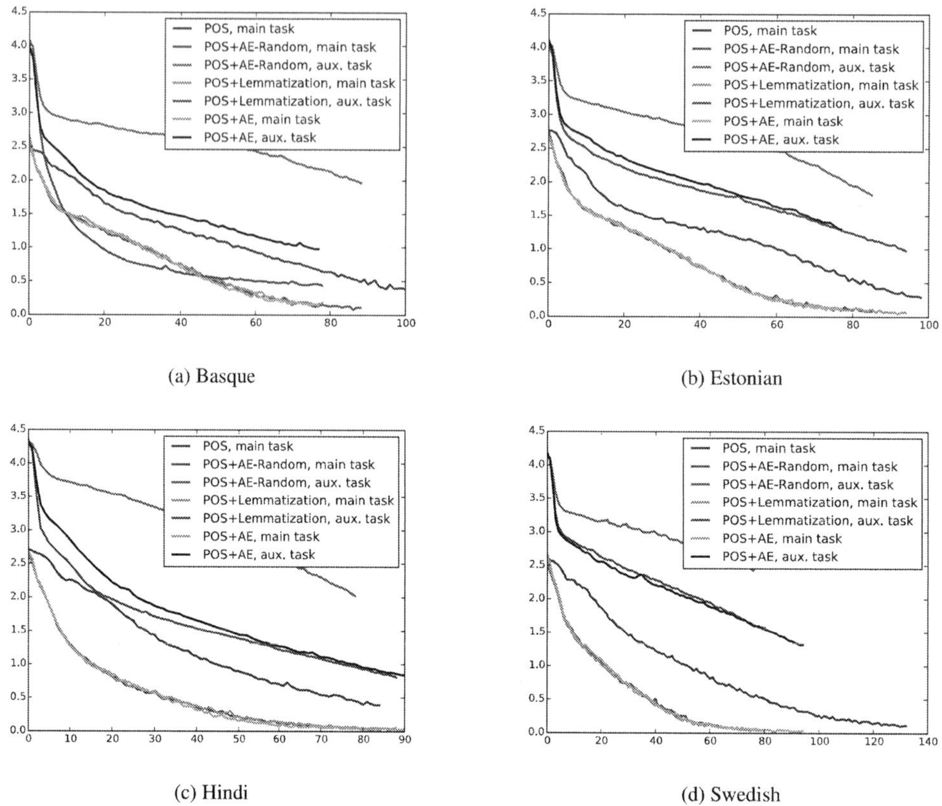

(a) Basque   (b) Estonian

(c) Hindi   (d) Swedish

Figure 2: Learning curve plots for four randomly selected languages, low setting.

gains for all investigated tasks, including POS. Finally, Gillick et al. (2016) present a multi-lingual model based on ideas from multi-task training, with each language constituting a separate task.

Multi-task learning in NLP. Neural networks make multi-task learning via (hard) parameter sharing particularly easy; thus, different task combinations have been investigated exhaustively. For sequence labeling, many combinations of tasks have been explored, e.g. by Søgaard and Goldberg (2016); Martínez Alonso and Plank (2017); Bjerva et al. (2016); Bjerva (2017a,b); Augenstein and Søgaard (2018). An analysis of task combinations is performed by Bingel and Søgaard (2017). Ruder et al. (2017) present a more flexible architecture, which learns what to share between the main and auxiliary tasks. Augenstein et al. (2017) combine multi-task learning with semi-supervised learning for strongly related tasks with different output spaces.

However, work on combining sequence labeling main tasks and sequence-to-sequence auxiliary tasks is harder to find. Dai and Le (2015) pretrain an LSTM as part of a sequence autoencoder on unlabeled data to obtain better performance on a sequence classification task. However, they report poor results for joint training. We obtain different results: even simple sequence-to-sequence tasks can indeed be beneficial for the sequence labeling task of low-resource POS tagging. This might be due to differences in the architectures or tasks.

Cross-lingual learning. Even though we do not employ cross-lingual learning in this work, we consider it highly relevant for low-resource settings and, thus, want to mention some important work here. Cross-lingual approaches have been used for a large variety of tasks, e.g., automatic speech recognition (Huang et al., 2013), entity recognition (Wang and Manning, 2014), language modeling (Tsvetkov et al., 2016), or parsing (Cohen et al., 2011; Søgaard, 2011; Naseem et al., 2012; Ammar et al., 2016). In the realm of sequence-to-sequence models, most work has been done for machine translation (Dong et al.,

8

2015; Zoph and Knight, 2016; Ha et al., 2016; Johnson et al., 2017). Another example is a character-based approach by Kann et al. (2017) for morphological generation.

8 Conclusion

We explored multi-task setups for training robust POS taggers for low-resource languages from small amounts of annotated data. In order to add additional character-level supervision into a hierarchical recurrent neural model, we introduced a novel network architecture. We considered different available types of external resources (word-lemma pairs, unlabeled corpora, or none) and employed corresponding auxiliary tasks (lemmatization, word autoencoding, or the artificial task of random string autoencoding) as well as varying amounts of auxiliary task data. While we did not find a systematic superior performance of models which were trained with lemmatization as an auxiliary task, the results confirmed our hypothesis that additional subword-level supervision improves POS taggers for resource-poor languages.

Acknowledgments

We would like to thank Paulina Grnarova and Rodrigo Nogueira for their helpful feedback. Isabelle Augenstein is partly supported by Eurostars grant Number E10138.

References

Željko Agić, Dirk Hovy, and Anders Søgaard. 2015. If all you have is a bit of the bible: Learning pos taggers for truly low-resource languages. In *ACL-IJCNLP*.

Roee Aharoni, Yoav Goldberg, and Yonatan Belinkov. 2016. Improving sequence to sequence learning for morphological inflection generation: The BIU-MIT systems for the SIGMORPHON 2016 shared task for morphological reinflection. In *SIGMORPHON*.

Waleed Ammar, George Mulcaire, Miguel Ballesteros, Chris Dyer, and Noah Smith. 2016. Many languages, one parser. *TACL*, 4:431–444.

Isabelle Augenstein, Sebastian Ruder, and Anders Søgaard. 2017. Multi-task learning of keyphrase boundary detection. In *ACL*.

Isabelle Augenstein and Anders Søgaard. 2018. Multitask learning of pairwise sequence classification tasks over disparate label spaces. In *NAACL*.

Dzmitry Bahdanau, Kyunghyun Cho, and Yoshua Bengio. 2015. Neural machine translation by jointly learning to align and translate. In *ICLR*.

Miguel Ballesteros, Chris Dyer, and Noah A Smith. 2015. Improved transition-based parsing by modeling characters instead of words with LSTMs. In *EMNLP*.

Chris Biemann. 2012. Unsupervised part-of-speech tagging. In *Structure Discovery in Natural Language*, pages 113–144. Springer.

Joachim Bingel and Anders Søgaard. 2017. Identifying beneficial task relations for multi-task learning in deep neural networks. In *EACL*.

Johannes Bjerva. 2017a. *One Model to Rule them all: Multitask and Multilingual Modelling for Lexical Analysis*. Ph.D. thesis, University of Groningen.

Johannes Bjerva. 2017b. Will my auxiliary tagging task help? Estimating auxiliary tasks effectivity in multi-task learning. In *NoDaLiDa*.

Johannes Bjerva, Barbara Plank, and Johan Bos. 2016. Semantic tagging with deep residual networks. In *COLING*.

Kyunghyun Cho, Bart van Merrienboer, Dzmitry Bahdanau, and Yoshua Bengio. 2014. On the properties of neural machine translation: Encoder–decoder approaches. In *SSST*.

Shay B Cohen, Dipanjan Das, and Noah A Smith. 2011. Unsupervised structure prediction with non-parallel multilingual guidance. In *EMNLP*.

Ryan Cotterell, Christo Kirov, John Sylak-Glassman, Géraldine Walther, Ekaterina Vylomova, Patrick Xia, Manaal Faruqui, Sandra Kübler, David Yarowsky, Jason Eisner, and Mans Hulden. 2017. The CoNLL-SIGMORPHON 2017 shared task: Universal morphological reinflection in 52 languages. In *CoNLL-SIGMORPHON*.

Andrew M Dai and Quoc V Le. 2015. Semi-supervised sequence learning. In *NIPS*.

Daxiang Dong, Hua Wu, Wei He, Dianhai Yu, and Haifeng Wang. 2015. Multi-task learning for multiple language translation. In *ACL-IJCNLP*.

Dan Gillick, Cliff Brunk, Oriol Vinyals, and Amarnag Subramanya. 2016. Multilingual language processing from bytes. In *NAACL-HLT*.

Sharon Goldwater and Tom Griffiths. 2007. A fully bayesian approach to unsupervised part-of-speech tagging. In *ACL*.

Thanh-Le Ha, Jan Niehues, and Alexander Waibel. 2016. Toward multilingual neural machine translation with universal encoder and decoder. *arXiv:1611.04798*.

Jui-Ting Huang, Jinyu Li, Dong Yu, Li Deng, and n Gong. 2013. Cross-language knowledge transfer using multilingual deep neural network with shared hidden layers. In *IEEE*.

Melvin Johnson, Mike Schuster, Quoc Le, Maxim Krikun, Yonghui Wu, Zhifeng Chen, Nikhil Thorat, Fernand a Vigas, Martin Wattenberg, Greg Corrado, Macduff Hughes, and Jeffrey Dean. 2017. Google's multilingual neural machine translation system: Enabling zero-shot translation. *TACL*, 5:339–351.

Katharina Kann, Ryan Cotterell, and Hinrich Schütze. 2017. One-shot neural cross-lingual transfer for paradigm completion. In *ACL*.

Katharina Kann and Hinrich Schütze. 2016. Single-model encoder-decoder with explicit morphological representation for reinflection. In *ACL*.

Diederik Kingma and Jimmy Ba. 2014. Adam: A method for stochastic optimization. *arXiv:1412.6980*.

Eliyahu Kiperwasser and Yoav Goldberg. 2016. Simple and accurate dependency parsing using bidirectional LSTM feature representations. *TACL*, 4:313–327.

John Lafferty, Andrew McCallum, and Fernando Pereira. 2001. Conditional random fields: Probabilistic models for segmenting and labeling sequence data. In *ICML*.

Shen Li, Joao V Graça, and Ben Taskar. 2012. Wiki-ly supervised part-of-speech tagging. In *EMNLP*.

Wang Ling, Chris Dyer, Alan W. Black, Isabel Trancoso, Ramon Fermandez, Silvio Amir, Luís Marujo, and Tiago Luís. 2015. Finding function in form: Compositional character models for open vocabulary word representation. In *EMNLP*.

Peter Makarov, Tatiana Ruzsics, and Simon Clematide. 2017. Align and copy: UZH at SIGMORPHON 2017 shared task for morphological reinflection. In *CoNLL-SIGMORPHON*.

Héctor Martínez Alonso and Barbara Plank. 2017. When is multitask learning effective? Semantic sequence prediction under varying data conditions. In *EACL*.

Thomas Müller, Helmut Schmid, and Hinrich Schütze. 2013. Efficient higher-order CRFs for morphological tagging. In *EMNLP*.

Tahira Naseem, Regina Barzilay, and Amir Globerson. 2012. Selective sharing for multilingual dependency parsing. In *ACL*.

Joakim Nivre, Johan Hall, Sandra Kübler, Ryan McDonald, Jens Nilsson, Sebastian Riedel, and Deniz Yuret. 2007. The CoNLL 2007 shared task on dependency parsing. In *EMNLP-CoNLL*.

Barbara Plank, Anders Søgaard, and Yoav Goldberg. 2016. Multilingual part-of-speech tagging with bidirectional long short-term memory models and auxiliary loss. *arXiv:1604.05529*.

Marek Rei. 2017. Semi-supervised multitask learning for sequence labeling. In *ACL*.

Sebastian Ruder, Joachim Bingel, Isabelle Augenstein, and Anders Søgaard. 2017. Sluice networks: Learning what to share between loosely related tasks. *arXiv:1705.08142*.

Helmut Schmid. 1995. Improvements in part-of-speech tagging with an application to German. In *SIGDAT*.

Anders Søgaard. 2011. Data point selection for cross-language adaptation of dependency parsers. In *ACL-HLT*.

Anders Søgaard and Yoav Goldberg. 2016. Deep multi-task learning with low level tasks supervised at lower layers. In *ACL*.

Ilya Sutskever, Oriol Vinyals, and Quoc V Le. 2014. Sequence to sequence learning with neural networks. In *NIPS*.

Charles Sutton, Michael Sindelar, and Andrew McCallum. 2006. Reducing weight undertraining in structured discriminative learning. In *NAACL*.

Oscar Täckström, Dipanjan Das, Slav Petrov, Ryan McDonald, and Joakim Nivre. 2013. Token and type constraints for cross-lingual part-of-speech tagging. *TACL*, 1:1–12.

Yulia Tsvetkov, Sunayana Sitaram, Manaal Faruqui, Guillaume Lample, Patrick Littell, David Mortensen, Alan W Black, Lori Levin, and Chris Dyer. 2016. Polyglot neural language models: A case study in cross-lingual phonetic representation learning. In *NAACL-HLT*.

Soroush Vosoughi, Prashanth Vijayaraghavan, and Deb Roy. 2016. Tweet2Vec: Learning tweet embeddings using character-level CNN-LSTM encoder-decoder. In *SIGIR*.

Mengqiu Wang and Christopher D Manning. 2014. Cross-lingual pseudo-projected expectation regularization for weakly supervised learning. *TACL*, 2:55–66.

Peilu Wang, Yao Qian, Frank K Soong, Lei He, and Hai Zhao. 2015. A unified tagging solution: Bidirectional LSTM recurrent neural network with word embedding. *arXiv:1511.00215*.

Zhilin Yang, Ruslan Salakhutdinov, and William Cohen. 2016. Multi-task cross-lingual sequence tagging from scratch. *arXiv:1603.06270*.

David Yarowsky, Grace Ngai, and Richard Wicentowski. 2001. Inducing multilingual text analysis tools via robust projection across aligned corpora. In *HLT*.

Barret Zoph and Kevin Knight. 2016. Multi-source
neural translation. In *NAACL-HLT*.

Training a Neural Network in a Low-Resource Setting on Automatically Annotated Noisy Data

Michael A. Hedderich[1,2]   **Dietrich Klakow**[1]

[1]Spoken Language Systems (LSV)
[2]Saarbrücken Graduate School of Computer Science
Saarland Informatics Campus, Saarland University, Saarbrücken, Germany
{mhedderich,dietrich.klakow}@lsv.uni-saarland.de

Abstract

Manually labeled corpora are expensive to create and often not available for low-resource languages or domains. Automatic labeling approaches are an alternative way to obtain labeled data in a quicker and cheaper way. However, these labels often contain more errors which can deteriorate a classifier's performance when trained on this data. We propose a noise layer that is added to a neural network architecture. This allows modeling the noise and train on a combination of clean and noisy data. We show that in a low-resource NER task we can improve performance by up to 35% by using additional, noisy data and handling the noise.

1   Introduction

For training statistical models in a supervised way, labeled datasets are required. For many natural language processing tasks like part-of-speech tagging (POS) or named entity recognition (NER), every word in a corpus needs to be annotated. While the large effort of manual annotation is regularly done for English, for other languages this is often not the case. And even for English, the corpora are usually limited to certain domains like newspaper articles. For tasks in low-resource areas there tend to be no or only few labeled words available.

Distant supervision and automatic labeling approaches are an alternative to manually creating labels. These exploit the fact that frequently large amounts of unannotated texts do exist in the targeted domain, e.g. from web crawls. The labels are then assigned using techniques like transferring information from high-resource languages (Das and Petrov, 2011) or simple look-ups in

knowledge bases or gazetteers (Dembowski et al., 2017). Once such an automatic labeling system is set up, the amount of text to annotate becomes nearly irrelevant, especially in comparison to manual annotation. Also, it is often rather easy to apply the system to different settings, e.g. by using a knowledge base in a different language.

However, while easily obtainable in large amounts, the automatically annotated data usually contains more errors than the manually annotated. When training a machine learning algorithm on such noisy training data, this can result in a low performance. Furthermore, the combination of noisy and clean training instances can perform even worse than just using clean data.

In this work, we present an approach to training a neural network with a combination of a small amount of clean data and a larger set of automatically annotated, noisy instances. We model the noise explicitly using a noise layer that is added to the network architecture. This allows us to directly optimize the network weights using standard techniques. After training, the noise layer is not needed anymore, removing any added complexity.

This technique is applicable to different classification scenarios and in this work, we apply it to an NER task. To obtain a non-synthetic, realistic source of noise, we use look-ups from gazetteers for automatically annotating the data. In the low-resource setting, we show the performance boost obtained from training with both clean and noisy instances and from handling the noise in the data. We also compare to another recent neural network noise-handling approach and we give some more insight into the impact of using additional noisy data and into the learned noise model.

Proceedings of the Workshop on Deep Learning Approaches for Low-Resource NLP, pages 12–18
Melbourne, Australia July 19, 2018. ©2018 Association for Computational Linguistics

2 Related Work

Existing work showed the importance of handling label noise. Zhu and Wu (2004) suggested that noise in labels tends to be more harmful than noise in features. Beigman and Beigman Klebanov (2009) showed that annotation noise in difficult instances can deteriorate the performance even on simple instances that would have been classified correctly in the absence of the hard cases.

Rehbein and Ruppenhofer (2017) presented a technique for detecting annotation noise in automatically labeled POS and NER tags in an active learning scheme. It requires, however, several sources of automatic annotations and human supervision. Similarly, Rocio et al. (2007) and Loftsson (2009) focused on detecting noisy instances in (semi-) automatically annotated POS corpora, leaving the correction to human annotators.

The model proposed by Bekker and Goldberger (2016) assumes that all clean labels pass through a noisy channel. One does only observe the noisy labels. The model of the noise channel, as well as the clean labels, are estimated using an EM algorithm. A neural network is then trained on the estimated labels. van den Berg (2016) applied this model to different tasks, obtaining small improvements on NER with automatically annotated data. A disadvantage of this approach is that the neural network needs to be retrained in every iteration of the EM algorithm, making the model difficult to scale to complex neural architectures.

Goldberger and Ben-Reuven (2017) transformed this model into an end-to-end trainable neural network by replacing the EM component with a noise adaptation layer. They experimented with simple image classification data and Dgani et al. (2018) applied it on the medical image domain. Both limit their approach to only using noisy data. Also, they just evaluate the effectiveness of their noise-handling method on simple synthetic noise (uniform and permutation). When applied to real-life scenarios, the noise might have a more complex structure.

In the image classification domain, several ideas have been proposed for estimating cleaned labels using a combination of clean and noisy labels. Fergus et al. (2009) employ a label propagation approach. Sukhbaatar et al. (2015) apply a noise model on top of a Convolutional Neural Network. Vahdat (2017) constructs an undirected graphical model to represent the relationship between clean and noisy labels. However, an additional source of auxiliary information is needed to infer clean from noisy labels. The approach presented by Veit et al. (2017) uses two components. A cleaning network learns to map noisy labels to clean ones. The second network is used to learn the actual image classification task from clean and cleaned labels. We compare our approach to this idea in the experiments.

3 Noise Layer

Given a clean dataset C consisting of feature and label tuples (x, y), we can construct a multi-label neural network softmax classifier

$$p(y = i|x; w) = \frac{\exp(u_i^T h(x))}{\sum_{j=1}^{k} \exp(u_j^T h(x))} \quad (1)$$

where k is the number of classes, h is a non-linear function or a more complex neural network and w are the network weights including the softmax weights u.

The noisy dataset N is a set of additional training instances. Following the approach of Goldberger and Ben-Reuven (2017), we assume that each originally clean (but unseen) label y went through a noise channel transforming it into the noisy label z. We only observe the noisy label, i.e. N consists of tuples (x, z).

The noise transformation from a clean label y with class i to a noisy label z with class j is modeled using a stochastic matrix

$$\theta(i, j) = p(z = i|y = j) = \frac{\exp(b_{ij})}{\sum_{l=1}^{k} \exp(b_{il})} \quad (2)$$

for $i, j \in \{1, ..., k\}$ and where b are learned weights. We call this the noise layer here. The probability for an observed, noisy label then becomes

$$p(z = j|x; w; \theta) =$$
$$\sum_{i=1}^{k} p(z = j|y = i; \theta)p(y = i|x; w) \quad (3)$$

for $(x, z) \in N$.

In contrast to the work by Goldberger and Ben-Reuven (2017), we also have access to clean data C. From this, we create two models, as illustrated in Figure 1. The base model without noise layer is trained on C and the noise model with the noise layer is trained on N. Both models share the same

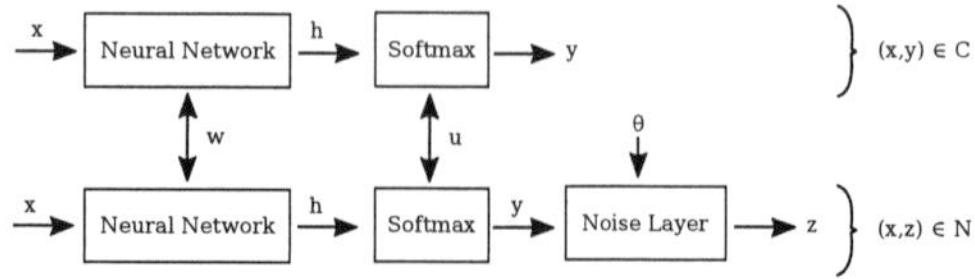

Figure 1: General architecture of the approach. Above is the base model trained on clean data C and predicting clean labels y. Below is the noise layer model trained on noisy label data N. The predicted labels y are transformed into the seen, noisy labels z using the noise layer.

network weights. The models are trained alternatingly, each for one epoch of its corresponding clean or noisy data. For prediction, the noise layer is removed and just the base model is used.

As stated by Goldberger and Ben-Reuven (2017), the initialization of θ is important. Since we have access to a small amount of clean data C, we use it for initializing the stochastic matrix. We assume that we can create noisy labels for the clean instances using the same process as for the noisy data N. We then initialize the weights of θ as

$$b_{ij} = \log\left(\frac{\sum_{t=1}^{|C|} 1_{\{y_t=i\}} 1_{\{z_t=j\}}}{\sum_{t=1}^{|C|} 1_{\{y_t=1\}}}\right) \qquad (4)$$

where z_t is obtained by creating a noisy label for $(x_t, y_t) \in C$.

4 Dataset and Automatic Annotation

Named Entity Recognition (NER) is the task of assigning phrases in a text an entity label. In the sentence

Only France backed Fischler's proposal.

the country *France* is of the entity class location and *Fischler* refers to a person. Creating training data for this task requires that each word in the text is labeled with its corresponding class. The effort to create a sufficiently large dataset might be too large for a low-resource language.

To tackle this problem, Dembowski et al. (2017) proposed to use external lists and gazetteers of entities to automatically label words in a training corpus. A list of person names can e.g be extracted from all of the entries appearing in Wikipedia's person category. Equipped with such lists for all

Class	Precision	Recall	F1
PER	48.09%	25.90%	33.67%
ORG	52.45%	10.02%	16.83%
LOC	56.76%	65.42%	60.78%
MISC	0.00%	0.00%	0.00%
Overall	53.31%	27.36%	36.16%

Table 1: Evaluation of the automatic labeling on the full English CoNLL-2003 training set (which we use as noisy dataset N).

entity classes, one can then label a text automatically. A word gets assigned a specific class if it appears in the corresponding entity list. A word or token that does not appear in any list gets assigned the null class "O". Additionally, simple heuristics help to resolve conflicts between lists and to remove some sources of errors. One might e.g. not label the day of the weeks as names, although *"Friday"* might be in the list of person names.

For this work, we use the English CoNLL-2003 NER corpus (Tjong Kim Sang and De Meulder, 2003). The dataset is labeled with the classes person (PER), location (LOC), organization (ORG), miscellaneous name (MISC) and the null class (O). It consists of a training, a development and a test set. To obtain a low-resource setting, we randomly sample a subset of the training set as clean data C. In the experiments, we vary this size between ca. 400 and 20000 words. The rest of the labels are removed from the training set.

We then label the whole training set using the method by Dembowski et al. (2017) in the version with heuristics. This approach of automatically labeling words allows to quickly obtain large amounts of labeled text. However, both precision and recall tend to be lower than for manually labeled corpora (cf. Table 1). It should be noted that the MISC class is not covered with this technique which is an additional source of noise in the automatically annotated data. We use this as our noisy data N.

5 Model Architectures and Training

In this section, we present the different model architectures we evaluated in our experiments and we give details on the training procedure.

For each instance, the input x is a sequence of words with the target word in the middle surrounded by 3 words from the left and from the right of the original sentence, e.g. x = *"coun-*

tries other than Britain until the scientific" where
"Britain" is the target word with label $y = $ LOC.
Sentence boundaries are padded. We encode the
words using the 300-dimensional GloVe vectors
trained on cased text from Common Crawl (Pennington et al., 2014).

The **base-model** uses a bidirectional LSTM
(Hochreiter and Schmidhuber, 1997) with state
size 300 to encode the input. Then a dense layer is
applied with size 100 and ReLU activation (Glorot et al., 2011). Afterwards, the softmax layer is
used for classification. This model is only trained
on the clean data C.

The **noise-model** is built upon the base model
and uses the noise layer architecture explained in
section 3. First, the model is trained without noise
layer for one epoch on the clean data. Then, we
alternate between training with the noise layer on
the noisy data and without the noise layer on the
clean, each for one epoch. Instead of training
on the full noisy corpus, we use a subsample $\tilde{N}$,
randomly picked in each epoch. This allows the
model to see many different noisy samples while
preventing the noise from being too dominant. In
section 6.2, we evaluate this effect.

For the **base-model-with-noise** we use the
same clean and noisy data but the noise layer is left
out, using only the base model architecture without an explicit noise-handling technique.

To evaluate the importance of the initialization
of the stochastic matrix θ, the **noise-model-with-identity-init** uses the same training approach and
data as the *noise-model*. However, θ is initialized
with the identity matrix instead of using formula
4.

The **noise-adaptation-model** uses the original
model of Goldberger and Ben-Reuven (2017). It
consists of the base model with the noise layer
and is trained on the whole noisy dataset in each
epoch. It does not use the clean data. For initializing θ, the base model is pretrained on the noisy
data and its predictions are used as an approximation to the clean labels.

We also compare to the recent work by Veit
et al. (2017). They train a noise cleaning component which learns to map from a noisy label and
a feature representation to a clean label. These
cleaned labels are then used for training of what
we call the base model. The authors did not report
specific layer sizes and their architecture is developed for an image classification task, which differs structurally from our NER dataset (e.g. their
label vector is much sparser). We, therefore, adapt
their concept to our setting. As feature representation, we use the output of the BiLSTM which
is projected to a 30-dimensional space with a linear layer. This is concatenated with the noisy label and used as input to the noise cleaning component. It is passed through a dense layer with
the same dimension as the label vector. The skip-connection and clipping are used as in their publication. We use the same training approach and
data as with the *noise-model*, replacing the step
where the noise layer is trained. Instead, in each
epoch the noise cleaning component is trained on
C and the corresponding noisy labels. The base
model is then trained on a cleaned version of $\tilde{N}$
and C. We call this the **noise-cleaning-model**.

All models are trained using cross-entropy loss,
except for the noise cleaning component of the
noise-cleaning-model which is trained with the absolute error loss like in the original paper. All
models are trained for 40 epochs and the weights
of the best performing epoch are selected according to the F1 score on the development set. Adam
(Kingma and Ba, 2015) is used for stochastic optimization.

6 Experiments and Evaluation

In this section, we report on our experiments and
their results. The training on noisy data as well
as the randomness in training neural networks in
general lead to a certain amount of variance in the
evaluation scores. Therefore, we repeat all experiments five times and report the average as well as
the standard error. To obtain meaningful results,
no noise is added to the test data.

6.1 Model Comparison

To simulate different degrees of low-resource settings, we trained the models on different amounts
of clean data. We vary the size between 407 labeled words (0.2% of the CoNLL-2003 training
data) and 20362 labeled words (10%) in six steps.
Since the noisy labels are easy to obtain, we use
the whole corpus N. The size of the random subsample $\tilde{N}$ in each epoch is set to the same size as
the clean data.

The results of this experiment are given in Figure 2. There is a general trend that the larger the
amount of clean data is, the lower the differences
between the models are. It seems that once we

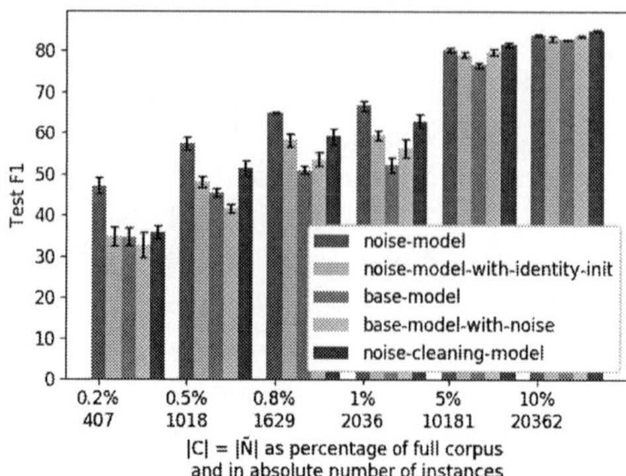

Figure 2: Evaluation results of the models. Experiments were run for different sizes of the clean data C and the per epoch randomly subsampled data $\tilde{N}$. The average F1 score on the test set is given over five runs. The error bars show two-times standard error in both directions.

have obtained enough clean training data, the additional noisy data cannot add much more information, even when cleaned. This is reminiscent of results from semi-supervised learning (e.g. in Nigam et al., 2006).

For the two settings with the lowest amount of data, the *base-model-with-noise* (which is trained on clean and noisy data without a noise channel) performs worst. For the four settings with more data, it is better than *base-model* (which is only trained on C). This could indicate that noisy labels do hurt the performance in low-resource settings. However, once a certain amount of clean training data is obtained, this is enough to cope with the noise to a certain degree and obtain improvements, even when the noise is not explicitly handled.

The models that do handle noise, outperform these baselines. When comparing *noise-model* and *noise-model-with-identity-init*, we see a large gap in performance. This shows the importance of a good initialization of the noise model θ in the low-resource setting.

The original *noise-adaptation-model* model by Goldberger and Ben-Reuven (2017) obtains an average F1 score of 38.8. This shows that a model purely trained on a large amount of automatically annotated data can be an alternative to a model trained on very few clean instances. However, the effect of cleaning noisy labels without access to any clean data seems limited, as the model cannot even reach the performance of either the *base-*

model trained on 1018 instances nor our *noise-model* on the smaller set of 407 instances.

The *noise-model* outperforms the *cleaning-model* in the four lower-resource settings while the latter performs slightly better in the two scenarios with more data. With its access to the features in the noise cleaning component, the *cleaning-model* might be able to model more complex noise transformations. However, it does not seem to be able to leverage this capability in a low-resource setting. In the low-resource settings, our *noise-model* is able to handle the noise well and it gains over ten points in F1 score over not using a noise-handling mechanism or only training on clean data.

6.2 Amount of Noisy Data

In this experiment, we evaluate the effect of using different amounts of noisy data during each epoch, i.e. we vary the size of the subsampled, noisy data $\tilde{N}$. We experiment with the *noise-model* and fix the amount of clean data C to 2036 labeled words (1% of the CoNLL-2003 training data). We choose $|\tilde{N}|$ as multiples of $|C|$ using factors 0.5, 1, 2, 10, 20, 30 and 50.

The results are given in Figure 3. One can see a trend that increasing the size of $\tilde{N}$ results in an improvement in F1 score. This holds until factor 5. Afterwards, the performance degrades again. This might indicate that the noisy data becomes too dominant and the cleaning effect of the noise layer is not able to mitigate it.

6.3 Learned Weights

Since, for evaluation purposes, we do have access to the clean labels of the whole training set, we can compare the noise that is in the noisy data to what the noise layer learned. Table 1 shows the evaluation of the automatically annotated labels on the training data. Figure 4 shows the stochastic matrix θ that was learned in one run of training the *noise-model* with $|C| = |\tilde{N}| = 2036$ labeled words (1% of the CoNLL-2003 training data).

One can see that the learned weight matrix represents a reasonable model of the noise. For the classes PER, ORG and MISC, the recall is very low in the noisy data and therefore the corresponding weights in the first column of the matrix are high: Instances (or a certain percentage of the probability mass) which the base model correctly classifies as PER/ORG/MISC, are mapped to the class O because this is the corresponding noisy label (indicated by the low recall). For the LOC

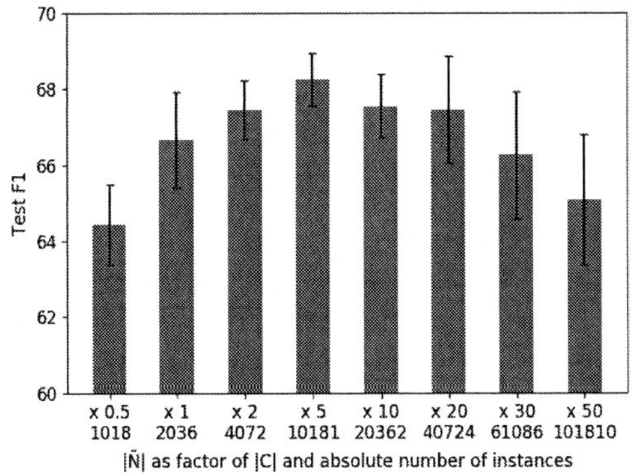

Figure 3: Evaluation results for varying the size of the per epoch randomly subsampled noisy data $\tilde{N}$. The *noise-model* was used and the amount of clean data C fixed to 2036 labeled words. The average F1 score on the test set is given over five runs. The error bars show two-times standard error in both directions.

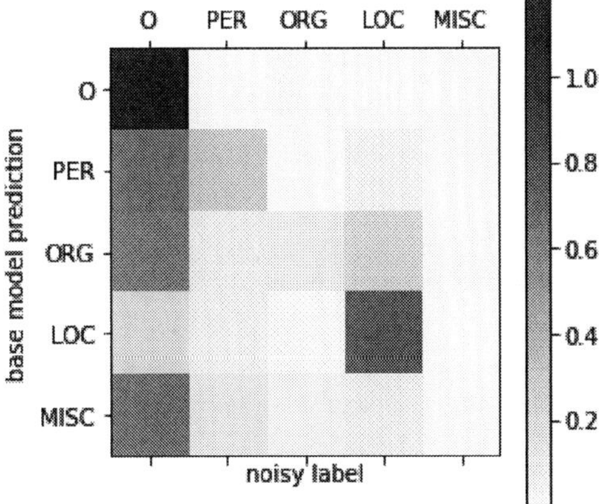

Figure 4: Representation of the noise transition weights θ learned in the noise layer. Each square is a value $\exp(\theta_{ij})$ where i is the vertical and j the horizontal index in the visualization.

class, the recall in the noisy labels is much higher and we see this reflected in the learned weights. The prominent weight is $\theta_{\text{LOC, LOC}}$, i.e. a prediction of the label LOC is mostly left unchanged because it tends to be correctly labeled in the noisy data.

7   Conclusions and Future Work

In this work, we presented a technique to train a neural network on a combination of clean and noisy annotations. We modeled the noise explicitly using a noise layer. We evaluated our approach on an NER task using real noise in the form of automatically annotated labels. We found that the probabilistic noise matrix learned is a useful model of the noise. In the low-resource setting where only a few manually annotated instances are available, we showed the improvements of up to 35% obtained from using additional, noisy data and handling the noise.

For future work, we want to experiment with different classification tasks and other sources of noisy data. We would also like to explore more complex noise models that are able to perform well both in low- and high-resource settings.

References

Eyal Beigman and Beata Beigman Klebanov. 2009. Learning with annotation noise. In *Proceedings of the Joint Conference of the 47th Annual Meeting of the ACL and the 4th International Joint Conference on Natural Language Processing of the AFNLP.*

Alan Joseph Bekker and Jacob Goldberger. 2016. Training deep neural-networks based on unreliable labels. In *IEEE International Conference on Acoustics, Speech and Signal Processing (ICASSP).*

Esther Maria van den Berg. 2016. Noisy label neural network approach to named entity recognition. Master's thesis, Rijksuniversiteit Groningen, Universität des Saarlandes.

Dipanjan Das and Slav Petrov. 2011. Unsupervised part-of-speech tagging with bilingual graph-based projections. In *Proceedings of the 49th Annual Meeting of the Association for Computational Linguistics: Human Language Technologies-Volume 1.*

Julia Dembowski, Michael Wiegand, and Dietrich Klakow. 2017. Language independent named entity recognition using distant supervision. In *Proceedings of Language and Technology Conference (LTC).*

Yair Dgani, Hayit Greenspan, and Jacob Goldberger. 2018. Training a neural network based on unreliable human annotation of medical images. In *IEEE International Symposium on Biomedical Imaging (ISBI).*

Rob Fergus, Yair Weiss, and Antonio Torralba. 2009. Semi-supervised learning in gigantic image collections. In *Advances in neural information processing systems.*

Xavier Glorot, Antoine Bordes, and Yoshua Bengio. 2011. Deep sparse rectifier neural networks. In *Proceedings of the Fourteenth International Conference on Artificial Intelligence and Statistics.*

Jacob Goldberger and Ehud Ben-Reuven. 2017. Training deep neural-networks using a noise adaptation layer. In *Int. Conference on Learning Representations (ICLR)*.

Sepp Hochreiter and Jürgen Schmidhuber. 1997. Long short-term memory. *Neural computation*, 9(8).

Diederik Kingma and Jimmy Ba. 2015. Adam: A method for stochastic optimization. In *International Conference on Learning Representations (ICLR)*.

Hrafn Loftsson. 2009. Correcting a pos-tagged corpus using three complementary methods. In *Proceedings of the 12th Conference of the European Chapter of the Association for Computational Linguistics*.

Kamal Nigam, Andrew McCallum, and Tom Mitchell. 2006. Semi-supervised text classification using em. *Semi-Supervised Learning*.

Jeffrey Pennington, Richard Socher, and Christopher D. Manning. 2014. Glove: Global vectors for word representation. In *Empirical Methods in Natural Language Processing (EMNLP)*.

Ines Rehbein and Josef Ruppenhofer. 2017. Detecting annotation noise in automatically labelled data. In *Proceedings of the 55th Annual Meeting of the Association for Computational Linguistics (Volume 1: Long Papers)*.

Vitor Rocio, Joaquim Silva, and Gabriel Lopes. 2007. Detection of strange and wrong automatic part-of-speech tagging. In *Progress in Artificial Intelligence*.

Sainbayar Sukhbaatar, Joan Bruna, Manohar Paluri, Lubomir D. Bourdev, and Rob Fergus. 2015. Training convolutional networks with noisy labels. In *ICLR Workshop track*.

Erik F Tjong Kim Sang and Fien De Meulder. 2003. Introduction to the conll-2003 shared task: Language-independent named entity recognition. In *Proceedings of the seventh conference on Natural language learning at HLT-NAACL*.

Arash Vahdat. 2017. Toward robustness against label noise in training deep discriminative neural networks. In *Advances in Neural Information Processing Systems*.

Andreas Veit, Neil Alldrin, Gal Chechik, Ivan Krasin, Abhinav Gupta, and Serge Belongie. 2017. Learning from noisy large-scale datasets with minimal supervision. In *The Conference on Computer Vision and Pattern Recognition (CVPR)*.

Xingquan Zhu and Xindong Wu. 2004. Class noise vs. attribute noise: A quantitative study. *Artificial Intelligence Review*, 22.

Multi-task learning for historical text normalization: Size matters

Marcel Bollmann, Anders Søgaard, Joachim Bingel
Dept. of Computer Science
University of Copenhagen
Denmark
`{marcel,soegaard,bingel}@di.ku.dk`

Abstract

Historical text normalization suffers from small datasets that exhibit high variance, and previous work has shown that multi-task learning can be used to leverage data from related problems in order to obtain more robust models. Previous work has been limited to datasets from a specific language and a specific historical period, and it is not clear whether results generalize. It therefore remains an open problem, *when* historical text normalization benefits from multi-task learning. We explore the benefits of multi-task learning across 10 different datasets, representing different languages and periods. Our main finding—contrary to what has been observed for other NLP tasks—is that multi-task learning mainly works when target task data is very scarce.

1 Introduction

Historical text normalization is the problem of translating historical documents written in the absence of modern spelling conventions and making them amenable to search by today's scholars, processable by natural language processing models, and readable to laypeople. In other words, historical text normalization is a text-to-text generation, where the input is a text written centuries ago, and the output is a text that has the same contents, but uses the orthography of modern-day language. In this paper, we limit ourselves to word-by-word normalization, ignoring the syntactic differences between modern-day languages and their historic predecessors.

Resources for historical text normalization are scarce. Even for major languages like English and German, we have very little training data for in-ducing normalization models, and the models we induce may be very specific to these datasets and not scale to writings from other historic periods—or even just writings from another monastery or by another author.

Bollmann and Søgaard (2016) and Bollmann et al. (2017) recently showed that we can obtain more robust historical text normalization models by exploiting synergies across historical text normalization datasets and with related tasks. Specifically, Bollmann et al. (2017) showed that multi-task learning with German grapheme-to-phoneme translation as an auxiliary task improves a state-of-the-art sequence-to-sequence model for historical text normalization of medieval German manuscripts.

Contributions We study *when* multi-task learning leads to improvements in historical text normalization. Specifically, we evaluate a state-of-the-art approach to historical text normalization (Bollmann et al., 2017) with and without various auxiliary tasks, across 10 historical text normalization datasets. We also include an experiment in English historical text normalization using data from Twitter and a grammatical error correction corpus (FCE) as auxiliary datasets. Across the board, we find that, unlike what has been observed for other NLP tasks, *multi-task learning only helps when target task data is scarce.*

2 Datasets

We consider 10 datasets from 8 different languages: German, using the Anselm dataset (taken from Bollmann et al., 2017) and texts from the RIDGES corpus (Odebrecht et al., 2016)[1]; English, Hungarian, Icelandic, and Swedish (from Pettersson, 2016); two versions of Slovene using different alphabets (Bohorič or Gaj; from Ljubešić

---

[1] `https://korpling.org/ridges/`

Proceedings of the Workshop on Deep Learning Approaches for Low-Resource NLP, pages 19–24
Melbourne, Australia July 19, 2018. ©2018 Association for Computational Linguistics

Dataset/Language		Time Period	Tokens			Source of Splits
			Train	Dev	Test	
DE$_A$	German (Anselm)	14th–16th c.	233,947	45,996	45,999	Bollmann et al. (2017)
DE$_R$	German (RIDGES)	1482–1652	41,857	9,712	9,587	–
EN	English	1386–1698	147,826	16,334	17,644	Pettersson (2016)
ES	Spanish	15th–19th c.	97,320	11,650	12,479	–
HU	Hungarian	1440–1541	134,028	16,707	16,779	Pettersson (2016)
IS	Icelandic	15th c.	49,633	6,109	6,037	Pettersson (2016)
PT	Portuguese	15th–19th c.	222,525	26,749	27,078	–
SL$_B$	Slovene (Bohorič)	1750–1840s	50,023	5,841	5,969	Ljubešić et al. (2016)
SL$_G$	Slovene (Gaj)	1840s–1899	161,211	20,878	21,493	Ljubešić et al. (2016)
SV	Swedish	1527–1812	24,458	2,245	29,184	Pettersson (2016)

Table 1: Historical datasets used in our experiments

et al., 2016); as well as Spanish and Portuguese texts from the Post Scriptum corpus (Vaamonde, 2017)[2].

For the Anselm dataset, we concatenate the individual training, development, and test sets from Bollmann et al. (2017) to obtain a single dataset. For RIDGES, we use 16 texts and randomly sample 70% of all sentences from each text for the training set, and 15% for the dev/test sets. The Spanish and Portuguese datasets consist of manually normalized subsets of the Post Scriptum corpus; here, we randomly sample 80% (train) and 10% (dev/test) of all sentences per century represented in the corpus. Dataset splits for the other languages are taken from Pettersson (2016) and Ljubešić et al. (2016).

We preprocessed all datasets to remove punctuation, perform Unicode normalization, replace digits that do not require normalization with a dummy symbol, and lowercase all tokens.

Table 1 gives an overview of all historical datasets, the approximate time period of historical texts that they cover, as well as the size of the dataset splits. Note that, to the best of our knowledge, the Spanish, Portuguese, and German RIDGES datasets have not been used in the context of automatic historical text normalization before.

Table 2 additionally gives some examples of historical word forms and their gold-standard normalizations from each of these datasets.[3]

3 Experimental setup

Model We use the same encoder–decoder architecture with attention as described in Bollmann et al. (2017).[4] This is a fairly standard model consisting of one bidirectional LSTM unit in the encoder and one (unidirectional) LSTM unit in the decoder. The input for the encoder is a single historical word form represented as a sequence of characters and padded with word boundary symbols; i.e., we only input single tokens in isolation, not full sentences. The decoder attends over the encoder's outputs and generates the normalized output characters.

Hyperparameters We use the same hyperparameters across all our experiments: The dimensionality of the embedding layer is 60, the size of the LSTM layers is set to 300, and we use a dropout rate of 0.2. We use the Adam optimizer (Kingma and Ba, 2014) with a character-wise cross-entropy loss. Training is done on mini-batches of 50 samples with early stopping based on validation on the individual development sets. The hyperparameters were set on a randomly selected subset of 50,000 tokens from each of the following datasets: English, German (Anselm), Hungarian, Icelandic, and Slovene (Gaj).

Multi-task learning Bollmann et al. (2017) also describe a multi-task learning (MTL) scenario where the encoder–decoder model is trained on two datasets in parallel. We perform similar experiments on pairwise combinations of our datasets.

---

[2]http://ps.clul.ul.pt

[3]Note that normalization guidelines differ between the datasets, and normalizations do not always constitute a modern word form—e.g. in the case of extinct lexemes—or the correct inflected form in the given context.

[4]The implementation is taken from: https://bitbucket.org/mbollmann/acl2017

DE$_A$	deſe wort ſpricht vnſer liber here iheſus criſtus czu eyme iczlychen menſchen	
	diese wort spricht unser lieber herr jesus christus zu einem ieteslichen menschen	
DE$_R$	ſeind ſẏ doch alle aufz den vier elementen gemiſchet vnd eins feüchter deñ das ander	
	sind sie doch alle aus den vier elementen gemischt und eins feuchter denn das andere	
EN	whan your graciouse erthely persoune from your inward spirit ys dessolued	
	when your gracious earthly person from your inward spirit is dissolved	
ES	anque tomeys mui mucho travajo tengola guardada pa quando dios sea servido	
	aunque toméis muy mucho trabajo téngola guardada para cuando dios sea servido	
HU	o zauoc éſmé felèmèluē kèzdènc ſirńoc èlmēnèc èzèkèt tolga ez a noemi azeɔt iouo	
	ő szavuk ismét felemelvén kezdének sírniuk elmenjek ezeket toldja ez a noémi azért jöve	
IS	þá sem hanz gödverk voru i og þá vrdu hanns gödverk miklu þýngre enn ill	
	þá sem hans góðverk voru í og þá urðu hans góðverk miklu þyngri en ill	
PT	cõ a poenetencia que lhe derão pera avisar aos snres do sancto oficio	
	com a penitência que lhe deram para avisar aos senhores do santo oficio	
SL$_B$	ter ne bodi nevéren zhe ſe zherna perſt premozhi tezhe od nje rjav mòk	
	ter ne bodi neveren če se črna prst premoči teče od nje rjav mok	
SL$_G$	in privéže na vsak konec niti drobtino kruha in verže vse kokóśem breskevno vkuhanje lovre	
	in priveže na vsak konec niti drobtino kruha in vrže vse kokošim breskvino vkuhanje lovre	
SV	blef av rätten afsagdt det en syyn och rådhgångh nu nästkommande wårdagh hållas	
	blev av rätten avsagt det en syn och rådgång nu nästkommande vårdag hållas	

Table 2: Examples of input tokens (first line) and reference normalization (second line) for each of the historical datasets.

The question we ask here is whether training on pairs of datasets can improve over training on datasets individually, which pairings yield the best results, and what properties of the datasets are most predictive of this. In other words, we are interested in *when* multi-task learning works.

In the multi-task learning setting, the two datasets—or "tasks"—share all parts of the encoder–decoder model except for the final prediction layer, which is specific to each dataset. This way, most parts of the model are forced to learn language-independent representations. This is different from Luong et al. (2015) and related work in machine translation, where typically only the encoder or the decoder is shared. We do not explore these alternatives here.

During training, we iterate over both our datasets in parallel in a random order, with each parameter update now being based on 50 samples from *each* dataset. Since datasets are of different sizes, we define an epoch to be a fixed size of 50,000 samples. Validation is performed for both datasets after each epoch, and model states are saved independently for each one if its validation accuracy improved. This means that even if the ideal number of epochs is different for the datasets, only the best state for each dataset will be used in the end. Training ends only after the validation accuracy for *each* dataset has stopped improving.

Sparse data scenario The training sets in our experiments range from ca. 25,000 to 230,000 tokens. Generally, historical text normalization suffers from scarce resources, and our biggest datasets are considered *huge* compared to what scholars typically have access to. Creating gold-standard normalizations is cumbersome and expensive, and for many languages and historic periods, it is not feasible to obtain big datasets. Therefore, we also present experiments on reduced datasets; instead of taking the full training sets, we only use the first 5,000 tokens from each one.

In this case, for multi-task learning, we combine the small target datasets with the *full* auxiliary datasets. This procedure mimics a realistic scenario: If a researcher is interested in normalizing a language for which no manually normalized resource exists, they could conceivably create a small batch of manual normalizations for this language and then leverage an existing corpus in another language using multi-task learning.

Dataset	Full		Sparse	
	Single	MTL	Single	MTL
DE$_A$	88.00	87.78	65.99	71.93
DE$_R$	86.05	87.81	70.04	74.25
EN	93.95	93.46	75.43	81.02
ES	94.41	94.32	82.50	86.59
HU	89.43	88.56	49.21	54.86
IS	84.83	86.67	69.52	72.73
PT	93.45	93.36	78.61	81.97
SL$_B$	90.12	91.81	82.39	86.35
SL$_G$	94.79	94.53	89.54	91.03
SV	88.48	89.90	79.24	82.14

Table 3: Normalization accuracy (in percent) using the full or sparse training sets, both for the single-task setup and the best-performing multi-task (MTL) setup.

4 Results

We evaluate our models using normalization accuracy, i.e., the percentage of correctly normalized word forms. Table 3 compares the accuracy scores of our single-task baseline models and for multi-task learning, in both the full and the sparse data scenario. For multi-task learning, we report the test set performance of the best target-auxiliary task pair combination, as evaluated on development data. Figure 1 visualizes the results for all pairwise combinations of the multi-task models; here, we show the error reduction of multi-task learning over our single-task baseline to better highlight by how much the MTL setup changes the performance.

Full datasets We make two observations about the results for the full data scenario (the left side of Fig. 1): (i) the usefulness of multi-task learning depends more on the dataset that is being evaluated than the one it is trained together with; and (ii) for most datasets, multi-task learning is *detrimental* rather than beneficial.

One hypothesis about multi-task learning is that its usefulness correlates with either synergistic or complementary properties of the datasets. In other words, it is conceivable that the performance on one dataset improves most with an MTL setup when it is paired with another dataset that is either (i) very similar, or (ii) provides an additional signal that is useful for, but not covered in, the first dataset. The results in Figure 1 show that

Auxiliary data	Accuracy
None	75.43
Best above	81.02
Twitter	81.72
FCE	78.53

Table 4: Normalization accuracy for English (sparse): Single and MTL from Table 3; and with non-historical auxiliary datasets (Twitter & FCE).

there can indeed be considerable variation depending on the exact dataset combination; e.g., the error reduction on Slovene (Bohorič) ranges from 5% (when paired with the Gaj dataset) to 33.2% (when paired with Swedish). At the same time, the question whether multi-task learning helps at all seems to depend mostly on the dataset being evaluated. With few exceptions, for most datasets, the error rate either always improves or always worsens, independently of the auxiliary task.

Considering the dataset statistics in Table 1, it appears that the *size of the training corpus* is the most important factor for these results. The four corpora that consistently benefit from MTL— German (RIDGES), Icelandic, Slovene (Bohorič), and Swedish—also have the smallest training sets, with about 50,000 tokens or less. For other tasks, different patterns have been observed (Martínez Alonso and Plank, 2017; Bingel and Søgaard, 2017); see Sec. 5.

Sparse datasets In the sparse data scenario where only 5,000 tokens are used for training (right side of Fig. 1), MTL almost always leads to improvements over the single-task training setup. This further confirms the hypothesis that *multi-task learning is beneficial for historical text normalization when the target task dataset is small*.

English with non-historical auxiliary data We also conduct a follow-up experiment on the (sparse) English dataset using a Twitter normalization dataset (Han and Baldwin, 2011) and a grammatical error corpus (Yannakoudakis et al., 2011) as auxiliary data. The results are presented in Table 4. Surprisingly, the Twitter dataset is actually more helpful than the best historical dataset; but of course, it is also in-language, unlike the historical datasets.

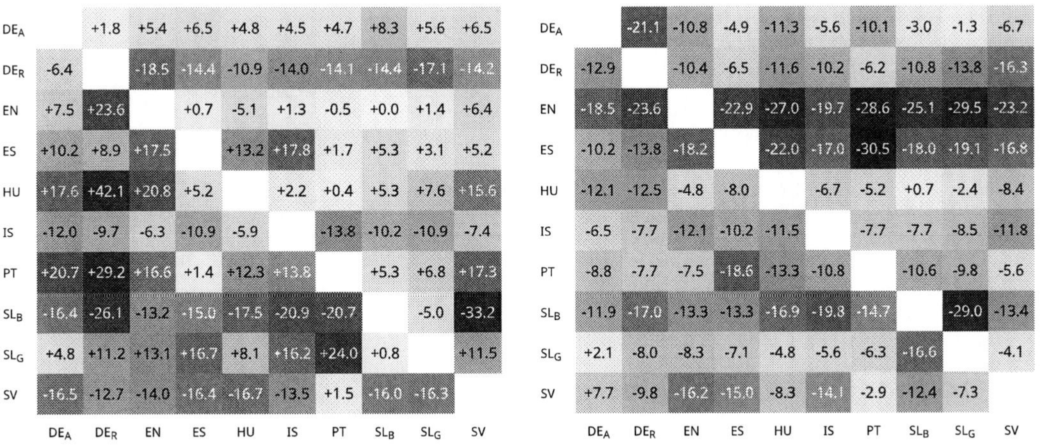

Left (full data):

	DE$_A$	DE$_R$	EN	ES	HU	IS	PT	SL$_B$	SL$_G$	SV
DE$_A$		+1.8	+5.4	+6.5	+4.8	+4.5	+4.7	+8.3	+5.6	+6.5
DE$_R$	-6.4		-18.5	-14.4	-10.9	-14.0	-14.1	-14.4	-17.1	-14.2
EN	+7.5	+23.6		+0.7	-5.1	+1.3	-0.5	+0.0	+1.4	+6.4
ES	+10.2	+8.9	+17.5		+13.2	+17.8	+1.7	+5.3	+3.1	+5.2
HU	+17.6	+42.1	+20.8	+5.2		+2.2	+0.4	+5.3	+7.6	+15.6
IS	-12.0	-9.7	-6.3	-10.9	-5.9		-13.8	-10.2	-10.9	-7.4
PT	+20.7	+29.2	+16.6	+1.4	+12.3	+13.8		+5.3	+6.8	+17.3
SL$_B$	-16.4	-26.1	-13.2	-15.0	-17.5	-20.9	-20.7		-5.0	-33.2
SL$_G$	+4.8	+11.2	+13.1	+16.7	+8.1	+16.2	+24.0	+0.8		+11.5
SV	-16.5	-12.7	-14.0	-16.4	-16.7	-13.5	+1.5	-16.0	-16.3	

Right (sparse data):

	DE$_A$	DE$_R$	EN	ES	HU	IS	PT	SL$_B$	SL$_G$	SV
DE$_A$		-21.1	-10.8	-4.9	-11.3	-5.6	-10.1	-3.0	-1.3	-6.7
DE$_R$	-12.9		-10.4	-6.5	-11.6	-10.2	-6.2	-10.8	-13.8	-16.3
EN	-18.5	-23.6		-22.9	-27.0	-19.7	-28.6	-25.1	-29.5	-23.2
ES	-10.2	-13.8	-18.2		-22.0	-17.0	-30.5	-18.0	-19.1	-16.8
HU	-12.1	-12.5	-4.8	-8.0		-6.7	-5.2	+0.7	-2.4	-8.4
IS	-6.5	-7.7	-12.1	-10.2	-11.5		-7.7	-7.7	-8.5	-11.8
PT	-8.8	-7.7	-7.5	-18.6	-13.3	-10.8		-10.6	-9.8	-5.6
SL$_B$	-11.9	-17.0	-13.3	-13.3	-16.9	-19.8	-14.7		-29.0	-13.4
SL$_G$	+2.1	-8.0	-8.3	-7.1	-4.8	-5.6	-6.3	-16.6		-4.1
SV	+7.7	-9.8	-16.2	-15.0	-8.3	-14.1	-2.9	-12.4	-7.3	

Figure 1: Percentage change of error of MTL over single-task models; rows are targets, columns auxiliary data. *Left:* full data; *right:* sparse data. Blue scores are improvements, reds increases in error.

5 Related work and conclusion

There has been considerable work on multi-task sequence-to-sequence models for other tasks (Dong et al., 2015; Luong et al., 2015; Elliott and Kádár, 2017). There is a wide range of design questions and sharing strategies that we ignore here, focusing instead on under what circumstances the approach advocated in (Bollmann et al., 2017) works.

Our main observation—that the size of the target dataset is most predictive of multi-task learning gains—runs counter previous findings for other NLP tasks (Martínez Alonso and Plank, 2017; Bingel and Søgaard, 2017). Martínez Alonso and Plank (2017) find that the label entropy of the auxiliary dataset is more predictive; Bingel and Søgaard (2017) find that the relative differences in the steepness of the two single-task loss curves is more predictive. Both papers consider sequence tagging problems with a small number of labels; and it is probably not a surprise that their findings do not seem to scale to the case of historical text normalization.

Acknowledgments

This research was supported by ERC Starting Grant LOWLANDS No. 313695 as well as by Trygfonden. Parts of this research were carried out by the first author at the Ruhr-Universität Bochum, Germany, supported by Deutsche Forschungsgemeinschaft (DFG), Grant DI 1558/4.

References

Joachim Bingel and Anders Søgaard. 2017. Identifying beneficial task relations for multi-task learning in deep neural networks. In *Proceedings of the 15th Conference of the European Chapter of the Association for Computational Linguistics: Volume 2, Short Papers*, pages 164–169. Association for Computational Linguistics.

Marcel Bollmann, Joachim Bingel, and Anders Søgaard. 2017. Learning attention for historical text normalization by learning to pronounce. In *Proceedings of the 55th Annual Meeting of the Association for Computational Linguistics (Volume 1: Long Papers)*, pages 332–344. Association for Computational Linguistics.

Marcel Bollmann and Anders Søgaard. 2016. Improving historical spelling normalization with bidirectional LSTMs and multi-task learning. In *Proceedings of COLING 2016, the 26th International Conference on Computational Linguistics: Technical Papers*, pages 131–139. The COLING 2016 Organizing Committee.

Daxiang Dong, Hua Wu, Wei He, Dianhai Yu, and Haifeng Wang. 2015. Multi-task learning for multiple language translation. In *Proceedings of the 53rd Annual Meeting of the Association for Computational Linguistics and the 7th International Joint Conference on Natural Language Processing (Volume 1: Long Papers)*, pages 1723–1732. Association for Computational Linguistics.

Desmond Elliott and Àkos Kádár. 2017. Imagination improves multimodal translation. In *Proceedings of the Eighth International Joint Conference on Natural Language Processing (Volume 1: Long Papers)*, pages 130–141. Asian Federation of Natural Language Processing.

Bo Han and Timothy Baldwin. 2011. Lexical normalisation of short text messages: Makn sens a #twitter. In *Proceedings of the 49th Annual Meeting of the Association for Computational Linguistics: Human Language Technologies*, pages 368–378. Association for Computational Linguistics.

Diederik P. Kingma and Jimmy Ba. 2014. Adam: A method for stochastic optimization. *CoRR*, abs/1412.6980.

Nikola Ljubešić, Katja Zupan, Darja Fišer, and Tomaž Erjavec. 2016. Normalising Slovene data: historical texts vs. user-generated content. In *Proceedings of the 13th Conference on Natural Language Processing (KONVENS 2016)*, volume 16 of *Bochumer Linguistische Arbeitsberichte*, pages 146–155, Bochum, Germany.

Minh-Thang Luong, Quoc V. Le, Ilya Sutskever, Oriol Vinyals, and Lukasz Kaiser. 2015. Multitask sequence to sequence learning. volume abs/1511.06114.

Héctor Martínez Alonso and Barbara Plank. 2017. When is multitask learning effective? semantic sequence prediction under varying data conditions. In *Proceedings of the 15th Conference of the European Chapter of the Association for Computational Linguistics: Volume 1, Long Papers*, pages 44–53. Association for Computational Linguistics.

Carolin Odebrecht, Malte Belz, Amir Zeldes, Anke Lüdeling, and Thomas Krause. 2016. RIDGES Herbology: designing a diachronic multi-layer corpus. *Language Resources and Evaluation*, pages 1–31.

Eva Pettersson. 2016. *Spelling Normalisation and Linguistic Analysis of Historical Text for Information Extraction*. Doctoral dissertation, Uppsala University, Department of Linguistics and Philology, Uppsala.

Gael Vaamonde. 2017. Userguide for digital edition of texts in P. S. Post Scriptum. Technical report. Translated by Clara Pinto.

Helen Yannakoudakis, Ted Briscoe, and Ben Medlock. 2011. A new dataset and method for automatically grading ESOL texts. In *Proceedings of the 49th Annual Meeting of the Association for Computational Linguistics: Human Language Technologies*, pages 180–189. Association for Computational Linguistics.

Compositional Language Modeling for Icon-Based Augmentative and Alternative Communication

Shiran Dudy   **Steven Bedrick**

Center for Spoken Language Understanding

Oregon Health & Science University

3181 S.W. Sam Jackson Park Rd.

Portland, Oregon, USA

`{dudy,bedricks}@ohsu.edu`

Abstract

Icon-based communication systems are widely used in the field of Augmentative and Alternative Communication. Typically, icon-based systems have lagged behind word- and character-based systems in terms of predictive typing functionality, due to the challenges inherent to training icon-based language models. We propose a method for synthesizing training data for use in icon-based language models, and explore two different modeling strategies.

1 Introduction

Individuals who experience speech and language impairments often are helped by Augmentative and Alternative Communication (AAC) techniques that facilitate the expression or comprehension of spoken or written language (Beukelman and Mirenda, 2005; American Speech Language Hearing Association et al., 2004; Fossett and Mirenda, 2007). Impairments may result from developmental disorders affecting speech and language (Cerebral Palsy, Down Syndrome, some forms of Autism Spectrum Disorder, etc.), or they may be caused by injury (stroke, traumatic brain injury, neurodegenerative diseases such as ALS, etc.). AAC interventions can take many forms, but a common goal is to provide users with a way to select symbols (words, phrases, etc.) for purposes of communication. The field of AAC groups interventions into "low-technology" (i.e., printed) or "high-technology" (i.e., computerized) devices; both are commonly used, and there are a number of factors that go in to the decision of which device to use (Iacono et al., 2011; Light and Drager, 2007). In some cases, devices produce speech (or written language) based on those selections, whereas in other cases, the goal of the device is to support a user in producing their own speech.

In some cases, the unit of selection may be icon-based rather than word- or character-based. This is particularly common in devices used by children or individuals with impaired literacy, but is also common in adult use. Icon-based systems can have higher selection speeds, and can be easier for individuals with neuromuscular impairments to operate; there are a wide variety of symbol sets and symbol-based communication systems used (Patel, 2011).

Computerized text-based AAC devices often include some form of word prediction using a language model (see (Vertanen and Kristensson, 2011; Garay-Vitoria and Abascal, 2006) for overviews of this area). Icon-based systems often do not employ predictive features.[1] In part, this is because they typically rely on direct-selection or other input modalities; another barrier, is a lack of relevant linguistic training data. To our knowledge, there are no corpora of language produced using icon-based AAC systems.

In the present work, we apply modern language modeling techniques to a large-vocabulary icon set commonly used in AAC applications, but for which we have no in-domain (or even in-vocabulary) training data. We are building our model as support for a brain-computer interface (Orhan et al., 2012). In this input modality, the user has very limited control over item selection, making accurate language modeling critical.

We propose a method to generate language models and evaluate their performance by experimenting with a process to generate a trainable language modeling corpus. We also share an experi-

---

[1] One notable exception to this trend is the system used in SymbolPath (Wiegand and Patel, 2012b), which uses semantic frames to attempt non-sequential symbol prediction (Wiegand and Patel, 2012a). This work, however, was limited to a specific and small icon set.

Proceedings of the Workshop on Deep Learning Approaches for Low-Resource NLP, pages 25–32

Melbourne, Australia July 19, 2018. ©2018 Association for Computational Linguistics

mental setup for a new language modeling architecture. Our contributions in this paper are:

- A proposed approach to synthesize a pseudo-corpus with which to learn language models from a corpus-less symbol set
- An experimental evaluation of the impact of various pieces of our corpus synthesis methodology on icon prediction accuracy
- A preliminary attempt to apply a novel language model architecture suitable for icon-based, open-vocabulary AAC applications

2   Symbolstix dataset

The Symbolstix (Clark, 1997) icon set is used in several commercial AAC applications. Each icon includes an image, and is associated with metadata information that textually describes the meaning assigned to the icon at hand. An image in this set can represent a single word, a phrase, or a syntactic modifier (such as "plural"). The images cover 48 major topics such as actions, technology, nature etc. They vary in meaning, demonstrating abstract concepts and tangible ones; they also present different levels of complexity and details. The metadata primarily describe the associated term the image corresponds to, its synonyms, and its translation to different languages.

The Symbolstix icon set was designed for use by communities who are in need of icon-based communication, such as children with communication disabilities, TBI patients, etc. One commercial application of the current icon-set is a newscast aimed at adult consumers; another is a communications platform for children with Cerebral Palsy. The set of 34k icons is in practice broad enough to reflect those needs. However, the creators of the system often do add new icons when requested by their user population.

Figure 1: Example icons: *afraid* and *bite leg*

On the left side of Figure 1 is an example of a single-word icon representing the term *afraid*. This icon's human-assigned topic category is "descriptives-feelings". Note that many icons are mapped to multiple synonyms. Synonyms of

this icon are: *eerie, fear, feared, fearful, fears, frightened, Halloween, scary, terrified, upset,* and *nervous.* As such, an icon's meaning is highly context-dependent.

The right-hand side icon in Figure 1 is an example of a two-word icon representing the concept *bite leg.* This icon's topic is of "actions". Synonyms of this icon are: "bad day" and "dog bite". As observed in Figure 1, the nature of the Symbolstix leans toward conversational concepts of spoken language, due to their intended use in AAC.

Symbolstix contains $34,837$ icons. $13,951$ of these icons are of a single word; several of these are duplicates[2], only $12,434$ of the single word icons are unique terms. In our experiment, to avoid redundancy, we used this set of unique terms. We chose the unique term-icon pair (from its non-unique group) that had the richest metadata and the highest overlap (within its group) to represent a concept. This step was essential to reduce complexity; however, it did introduce a limitation to our approach, which we discuss in section 5.

Notably, the Symbolstix corpus comes with no dataset that demonstrates the intended usage of icons to construct a proper sentence. Ideally, we would use a dataset of icon sentences for language modeling, as it would enable learning icon sequences and by that to infer the language rules from its patterns. In the next section, we describe how we were able to overcome that obstacle.

3   Experimental Setup

As mentioned in Section 2, the Symbolstix data set of icons has no sentence-like corpus from which icon sequences can be readily learned to form a language model of icons. We attempted to synthesize an icon corpus by beginning with a textual corpus, and "projecting" our icons into the text space using pre-trained word embeddings using the methodology described below. Since each icon is accompanied by metadata containing human-edited synonym lists, it was natural to represent icons as some composition of their synonyms in a vector space.

In this manner, we embedded our icons in text, and created pseudo-sequences ("icon sentences"). This solution is not without problems, first among them the issue is that our icon sentences may not

---

[2]A single lexical item may be represented several times; for example, there are several variants of "glue", with different shapes of bottles and patterns of labels.

represent realistic examples of how the Symbolstix icons are meant to be used. Rather, they might instead represent the icons as subjected to the language conventions found in oral or written language. For example comparing a possible icon sequence to the English language might look like:

Icon: *<I> <go> <here> <past>*
English: *<I> <went> <here>*, or
English: *<the> <dogs> <are> <at> <home>*
Icon: *<the> <dog> <plural> [<be> optional]
<at> <home>*

Some of the terms may disappear in translation, while others are added.

Another question is whether it is possible to fully represent an icon as the sum of its synonyms; or, put another way, whether the ways in which an icon's synonyms are used in written language can capture the totality of an icon's meaning. For example, the icon in figure 1 does not precisely mean "afraid", but rather refers to a more general concept. This is why we chose to explore a compositional approach to representing icon meaning in a continuous space. Finally, how should we handle sentences in our textual data set that are not fully representable using icons from Symbolstix?

Data Preprocessing

Icon Representation: In order to construct an icon language model, we needed to find a way to represent our icon vocabulary in a continuous embedding space (following the lead of Kiros et al. (2015)). Lacking a corpus that included icons, we were unable to directly train "icon embeddings" from data. Instead, we attempted to "project" our icons into a word embedding space.

We experimented with two different approaches of word embedding (see section 4), and, for each icon, generated icon embeddings by averaging[3] the word embeddings of the icon's synonyms (as specified by the Symbolstix metadata). Note that a different choice of icon set would have resulted in a different embedding space and language model. However, this basic approach describes a generic process to produce models form a corpus-less symbol-set, and should translate to other situations.

Textual Datasets: We next took a textual corpus (see section 4), and identified terms that could be replaced with icon embeddings. In this work, we relied on a relatively simple strategy of mechanically substituting icons for words based on

their Symbolstix metadata. In other words, instances of the word "wetland" in the corpus would be replaced by the icon with "wetland" in its list of synonyms or descriptor terms. Note that this icon's embedding would contain information about other words associated with that icon (e.g. "swamp"). We discuss some practical considerations around polysemous words and icons in section 4. This step forms a dataset of embedding sequences, which we then used as a corpus for learning a language model. The resulting corpus was then fully representable by embeddings (both of the words and icons).

Training

For our language model, we used a standard RNN architecture with two hidden LSTM layers, a linear, and a final softmax layer that predicts the term's index, trained with cross entropy loss function (seen in Equation 1). The model's input is of the generated embeddings and as such contained no explicit embedding layer.

$$L_i = \sum_{j \epsilon J} T(i,j) \log(P(i,j)). \qquad (1)$$

The icons in this project are aimed at patients who would use them as a means to communicate. It is very likely that the icon language that would be formed by these patients would share similar characteristics with spontaneous speech or informal language since this is the type of communication we have with a caregiver, family member, or a friend. Knowing this, we used the SubtlexUS (Brysbaert and New, 2009) corpus (made up of subtitles from movies and television) as a proxy for a corpus of spontaneous speech that contained $6,043,188$ sentences.[4]

Model Evaluation

We evaluated our language model using three different metrics:

- Mean Reciprocal Rank (MRR) of the "correct" predicted icon as seen in Equation 2

$$MRR = \frac{1}{|Q|} \sum_{i \epsilon Q} \frac{1}{rank_i}, \qquad (2)$$

Q represents the token events of the target. The choice of MRR metric was to internally

---

[3]We also experimented with summation, and observed no meaningful difference.

[4]See (Vertanen and Kristensson, 2011) for an extensive discussion on issues surrounding corpus selection for AAC applications.

look at the rank of the target, rather than to binary classify it for whether it was accurately predicted in the first rank.

- Accuracy@k: The percentage of predictions in which the "correct" icon was within the top k predictions. The choice in ACC@k was to inform about the quality of the prediction generated by the models. We have chosen ACC@1 to crudely understand whether the first choice was correct, and ACC@10 to get a sense of the prediction quality given that a user may be able to choose from a limited list (depending on the user interface), and also to model the notion that different users may choose different words in a simialr context (and so there is not a single correct word in reality).

4   Experiments

We performed three sets of experiments. The first explored the effect of different approaches to word embedding, the second explored the effects of either including or excluding non-icon terms in model training, and the third looked at the effects of other (non-Subtlex) text corpora. For both approaches to word embedding, we used pre-trained word vectors. The pretrained set is the source for generating the icon embeddings.

Both the icon and the pretrained embeddings replace the terms in the textual data with their corresponding vectors to generate an embedding corpus. All our experiments contained the same number of pretrained vectors as well as icon vectors. If both vector sets contained the same term, the icon embedding was used. The textual dataset was tokenized and punctuation was removed. Each of these experiments was held in a 5 fold cross validation fashion. The process to generate the corpus from which language models are learned is described in Figure 2.

This process shows also the three different modules we experimented with: the pretrained corpus, which forms the icon embeddings; the icon set that forms (with or with out the pretrained set (therefore the 'switch' between pretrained embeddings to textual dataset)) the textual embedding; and the textual dataset that provides the sequences of symbols to generate the textual embedding.

Experiment 1: Pretrained Vectors
The Pretrained embeddings in our experiment are used both to construct the icon representations and

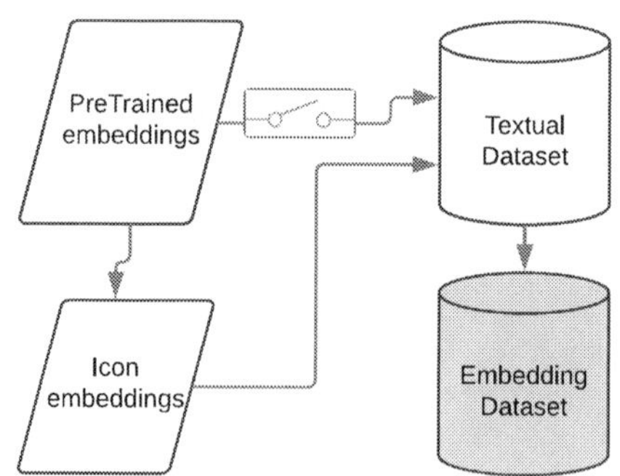

Figure 2: Block diagram to generate training set for language modeling

to represent the textual corpus. In our setting we have explored the Global Vectors for Word Representation (Glove) (Pennington et al., 2014) set consisting of 400,000 uncased entries and trained on Wikipedia 2014 and Gigaword version 5 ($\approx$6B tokens) with 50 embedding dimensions, and compared it to Context2Vec (c2v) (Melamud et al., 2016) trained on ukWaC corpus and MSCC ($\approx$2B + $\approx$50M tokens) consisting of 160,563 uncased entries, with 600 embedding dimensions. To maintain a controlled environment the textual dataset remained fixed, the vocabulary of pretrained token types was identical (n=69,840) as well as the icon list (n=6,934 term types) irrespective of the dataset used. A term in the dataset was prioritized to be replaced with an icon term first, then if not found, with an icon synonym, with a pretrained representation, and finally, provided no alternative, a term was replaced with an *<unk>* vector representation.

metric	c2v	Glove
MRR	0.85 (0.00)	0.85 (0.00)
ACC@1 (%)	50.99 (0.03)	49.29 (0.04)
ACC@10 (%)	90.51 (0.01)	90.29 (0.01)

Table 1: Effect of word embedding method

Table 1 contains the experimental results of evaluations run on models trained with Glove and c2v vectors, averaged across five folds of cross-validation on the SubtlexUS dataset.

After controlling for the number of icon- and pretrained-term types as well as for the textual corpus, Table 1 shows that there are no meaningful differences resulted from the pretrained vectors type. The dataset the vectors were trained on as well as the method by which the vectors were generated had no observable impact on the language model performance.

While Experiment 1 covers one aspect of comparing differences between different word embeddings, when choosing a pretrained set of vectors to use and generate icons from, there may be additional considerations. The coverage of the pretrained set is essential to produce icon representations, but also is important for terms in the textual dataset that cannot be represented with icons (which are then replaced with a pretrained vector if found) as described in Experiment 1. The pretrained set coverage with regards to the icon set is measured not only by the total number of icon representations that were generated from the pretrained set, but also by how well each icon captures the broad meaning it stands for. Since each icon is likely to have its name and synonyms composed together to represent it (as described in 3 in Data Preprocessing part), an optimal pretrained set would contain representations for all these terms. As for the textual dataset, an optimal coverage of the text with the pretrained list ideally would consist of a large number of term types, but also term events that appear in the dataset.

Experiment 2: Icon Symbols Constraint

Ideally, the corpus to learn language models from would consist of the icon vocabulary solely since the goal is to construct an Icon language model. We therefore, experimented with transforming our synthetic corpus to *only* include terms representable using icon vectors ("pure") and compared LM and prediction accuracy with the original, "non-pure" results. We used Glove and c2v vectors in our experiment presented in Table 2.

Table 2 describe an averaged five fold cross validation experiment of SubtlexUS with icon only embeddings referred by the "pure" experiment.

metric	c2v	Glove
MRR	0.33 (0.00)	0.33 (0.00)
ACC@1 (%)	46.79 (0.06)	45.72 (0.06)
ACC@10 (%)	54.92 (0.01)	54.29 (0.04)

Table 2: Effect of Icon embedding representation on SubtlexUS mean(standard deviation)

Table 2 describes a similar pattern to Table 1 as there was no meaningful change in the final icon language models' performances due to the "pure"

condition. We do note that there was a slight advantage to c2v embeddings which seemed to be predicting more correctly the target.

The "pure" condition resulted in a relatively smaller prediction accuracy. On the one hand, this may be surprising evidence, as it is reasonable to think that a smaller and more focused vocabulary set would result in an improved language model performance. We assume that the reduction in vocabulary size caused as a result of employing icons solely created short, sparse, and uncommon patterns of sequences, which limited the models' ability to learn and predict accurately.

Under the "pure" condition, the model vocabulary consists solely of the icon set itself, whereas in the "non-pure" condition, the model vocabulary consists of the icon set as well as the pretrained embeddings together with *<unk>* terms. While we can not directly compare the two experiments (1 and 2) we can share our considerations when choosing to generate language models purely based on icons.

To support our explanation for Table 2 interpretation, we conducted a qualitative test and looked into to the actual sentences produced by the icons in isolation, asking whether these sentences created "meaningful" (or at least useful) messages for LM training.. This might be helpful to get a deeper perspective on the corpus created and assist in making design choices. Here is an example:
"non-pure": *<your> <warning> <did> <not> <work>*
"pure": *<your> <warning> <not> <work>*
Arguably, the main message was conveyed in this sentence, while in the following:
"non-pure": *<they> <did> <n't> <use> <mud> <they> <used> <sod>*
"pure": *<they> <use> <they>*
the essence is gone. While it is not feasible to qualitatively look at every sentence, one may consider comparing the amount of tokens prior to elimination and post, under the assumption that the greater the loss, the more likely that the quality of solely using the icon-set becomes a concern.

We would like to note that in Experiment 2 in particular, we used the same simulated "icon language" for both training and evaluation. An ideal evaluation of our approach to producing synthetic in-domain training data would have been evaluating the language models trained on simulated icon language on "real" text composed using icons. As we did not have such a useful resource, it is important to observe this as a limitation of the current experiment.

Experiment 3: Textual Corpus

In our system, the role of the textual corpus is to provide the language model with training data regarding patterns of word ("icon") use. Ideally, we would use a corpus made of symbols that represent the type of content and structure an AAC user would produce. Finding an AAC-oriented corpus that would be big enough to train was a hurdle, and so for our previously-described experiments, we relied on SubtlexUS. While not ideal, this corpus was closer to spontaneous speech than, say, a newswire corpus would have been, and featured smaller and more manageable sentences that we hoped would withstand being converted to pseudo-icon representations.

That said, we did wish to investigate the utility of using an existing corpus that was designed to be closer to AAC-style speech. Vertanen and Kristensson (2011) produced such a corpus, consisting of 6,142 sentences produced by Amazon Mechanical Turk users who were paid to generate plausible sentences and to evaluate the plausibility of other sentences generated by other workers.

This corpus, while valuable, was too small for use with our language modeling approach. Following Vertanen and Kristensson's insight that "short text" such as that seen in online media such as Twitter, etc. might be a good proxy for true AAC-style speech, we therefore mixed the AAC-style corpus with second corpus, this one consisting of modified SMS messages. The second corpus was from Chen and Kan (2013) and consisted of 18,042 SMS messages, and was originally constructed for experiments in text normalization. As such, it includes messages written in heavily-abbreviated forms as well as "cleaned up" versions of each message, written in something approximating "standard" English orthography. We used this subset of the corpus in the hopes that its short, informal, and speech-like sentences would complement the AAC-style corpus. Our goal was to assemble a corpus containing language that is as close as possible to what would be produced by actual users of an AAC system. We then repeated the language modeling experiments conducted earlier on this hybrid corpus, using identical procedures and evaluation metrics.

Table 3 and 4 tell a similar story to one an-

metric	c2v	Glove
MRR	0.38 (0.00)	0.33 (0.01)
ACC@1 (%)	56.41 (0.52)	47.13 (2.81)
ACC@10 (%)	60.44 (0.42)	54.51 (2.37)

Table 3: Textual corpus (AAC-SMS) mean(standard deviation)

metric	c2v	Glove
MRR	0.37 (0.01)	0.34 (0.00)
ACC@1 (%)	53.25 (2.11)	47.73 (1.46)
ACC@10 (%)	59.06 (1.29)	56.00 (1.40)

Table 4: Textual corpus (AAC-SMS/pure) mean(standard deviation)

other: the models trained using c2v embeddings outperformed the models that used Glove embeddings, which is different from what we observed in the previous experiments— though with this corpus, the overall performance numbers were much lower than with the original, larger corpora. The reason for overall low performance was probably due to the very small size of the AAC-SMS corpus, and possible overfitting as a result. Digging more deeply into our data, we examined the individual cross-validation results at the fold level, thinking that perhaps the results were unstable due to the relatively small data set which indeed seem to be the case.

Nevertheless, in an attempt to indirectly evaluate different models, while the AAC experiments had substantially higher variance across folds than did the SubtlexUS experiments, the differences between the two approaches do appear to be real. Ultimately, we note that the substantial difference in corpus size between SubtlexUS and our AAC-SMS corpus make it difficult to draw any firm conclusions, and investigating this issue further will be a component of our future work in this area.

5 Conclusions

This work is a first step towards the development of language models for an icon set that has no corresponding corpus, but there remains much to be done. One limitation of this work is that, even after being projected into an icon space, our synthetic training data is somewhat different from actual icon-based language produced by AAC users. That said, we did try to overcome this limitation by experimenting with a corpus designed to be much closer to actual AAC-style language, though at a substantial cost in terms of corpus size. This is a common problem in AAC research in general, and our immediate next steps will focus on developing more naturalistic training corpora (following the lead of Vertanen and Kristensson (2011), who faced similar challenges).

Another important limitation is that we have not solved the problem of icons that represent multiword expressions or phrases. This will be a major area our future work, for two reasons. First, many important icons fall into this category. Second, one of the advantages of icon-based AAC is increased speed of communication, and collapsing multi-word expressions to a single icon would enable substantial improvements.

A second area of future work will look at ways to capture and express morphology. Our icon set includes icons that can be used to indicate tense, plurality, etc., but our current approach to corpus processing and term substitution/composition does not take advantage of such information. We intend to explore ways to directly represent morphological/inflectional information in the input side of our models, and in doing so make better use of our icon system.

A final limitation of this work is that our approach to selecting icons had the unfortunate side effect of ignoring polysemy: the set of icons that we worked with here was restricted to a single sense of polysemous words. This means that some possibly-useful icons were excluded, which could have consequences for anybody actually using our system for communication. Consider the word "cheer", which can be either a verb or a noun, and in both cases has multiple meanings. There are several icons in Symbolstix that capture different usages of the word, but our current approach only uses one. This will be another active area of future work, and we expect our solution to this problem to tie in with our solution to the issue of multiword expressions.

Our evaluations thus far have been system-oriented, and have tried to measure the model's performance. Our MRR and accuracy results have provided us with an internal view for where our models were performing as desired as well as identified areas where they fall short. The next step will be to integrate our language model with the rest of our AAC platform and begin working with real end-users. We anticipate that this will guide much of our future work on this problem.

Acknowledgments

We thank the anonymous DeepLo workshop reviewers for their valuable feedback and comments. We also thank our clinical collaborators in OHSU's Institute on Development & Disability: Betts Peters, Brandon Eddy, and Dr. Melanie Fried-Oken, as well as our collaborators at Northeastern University, in the laboratories of Drs. David Smith and Deniz Erdogmus. Research reported in this paper was supported by the National Institute on Deafness and Other Communication Disorders of the NIH under awards R01DC009834 and R56DC015999.

References

American Speech Language Hearing Association et al. 2004. Roles and Responsibilities of Speech-Language Pathologists with Respect to Augmentative and Alternative Communication: Technical Report .

David R. Beukelman and Pat Mirenda. 2005. *Augmentative & Alternative Communication: Supporting Children & Adults with Complex Communication Needs*. Paul H. Brookes Publishing Co., 3rd edition.

Marc Brysbaert and Boris New. 2009. Moving Beyond Kučera and Francis: A Critical Evaluation of Current Word Frequency Norms and the Introduction of a New and Improved Word Frequency Measure for American English. *Behavior Research Methods* 41(4):977–990.

Tao Chen and Min-Yen Kan. 2013. Creating a live, public short message service corpus: the nus sms corpus. *Language Resources and Evaluation* 47(2):299–335.

Jacquie Clark. 1997. *Symbolstix*. News 2 You. https://www.n2y.com/symbolstix-prime.

Brenda Fossett and Pat Mirenda. 2007. Augmentative and Alternative Communication. *Handbook of Developmental Disabilities* pages 330–348.

Nestor Garay-Vitoria and Julio Abascal. 2006. Text prediction systems: a survey. *Universal Access in the Information Society* 4(3):188–203.

Teresa Iacono, Katie Lyon, and Denise West. 2011. Non-Electronic Communication Aids for People with Complex Communication Needs. *International Journal of Speech-Language Pathology* 13(5):399–410.

Ryan Kiros, Yukun Zhu, Ruslan R Salakhutdinov, Richard Zemel, Raquel Urtasun, Antonio Torralba, and Sanja Fidler. 2015. Skip-Thought Vectors. In *Advances in Neural Information Processing Systems*. pages 3294–3302.

Janice Light and Kathryn Drager. 2007. AAC Technologies for Young Children with Complex Communication Needs: State of the Science and Future Research Directions. *Augmentative and Alternative Communication* 23(3):204–216.

Oren Melamud, Jacob Goldberger, and Ido Dagan. 2016. context2vec: Learning Generic Context Embedding with Bidirectional LSTM. In *Proceedings of The 20th SIGNLL Conference on Computational Natural Language Learning*. pages 51–61.

U. Orhan, K. E. Hild, D. Erdogmus, B. Roark, B. Oken, and M. Fried-Oken. 2012. Rsvp Keyboard: An EEG Based Typing Interface. In *2012 IEEE International Conference on Acoustics, Speech and Signal Processing (ICASSP)*. pages 645–648.

R. Patel. 2011. Message Formulation, Organization, and Navigation Schemes for Icon-Based Communication Aids. In *2011 Annual International Conference of the IEEE Engineering in Medicine and Biology Society*. pages 5364–5367.

Jeffrey Pennington, Richard Socher, and Christopher Manning. 2014. Glove: Global Vectors for Word Representation. In *Proceedings of the 2014 Conference on Empirical Methods in Natural Language Processing (EMNLP)*. pages 1532–1543.

Keith Vertanen and Per Ola Kristensson. 2011. The imagination of crowds: Conversational aac language modeling using crowdsourcing and large data sources. In *Proceedings of the Conference on Empirical Methods in Natural Language Processing*. Association for Computational Linguistics, Stroudsburg, PA, USA, EMNLP '11, pages 700–711. http://dl.acm.org/citation.cfm?id=2145432.2145514.

Karl Wiegand and Rupal Patel. 2012a. Nonsyntactic word prediction for aac. In *Proceedings of the Third Workshop on Speech and Language Processing for Assistive Technologies*. Association for Computational Linguistics, Stroudsburg, PA, USA, SLPAT '12, pages 28–36. http://dl.acm.org/citation.cfm?id=2392855.2392860.

Karl Wiegand and Rupal Patel. 2012b. Symbolpath: A continuous motion overlay module for icon-based assistive communication. In *Proceedings of the 14th International ACM SIGACCESS Conference on Computers and Accessibility*. ACM, New York, NY, USA, ASSETS '12, pages 209–210. https://doi.org/10.1145/2384916.2384957.

Multimodal Neural Machine Translation for Low-resource Language Pairs using Synthetic Data

Koel Dutta Chowdhury
ADAPT Centre
School of Computing
Dublin City University
Dublin, Ireland
koel.chowdhury@adaptcentre.ie

Mohammed Hasanuzzaman
ADAPT Centre
School of Computing
Dublin City University
Dublin, Ireland
mohammed.hasanuzzaman@adaptcentre.ie

Qun Liu
ADAPT Centre
School of Computing
Dublin City University
Dublin, Ireland
qun.liu@adaptcentre.ie

Abstract

In this paper, we investigate the effectiveness of training a multimodal neural machine translation (MNMT) system with image features for a low-resource language pair, Hindi and English, using synthetic data. A three-way parallel corpus which contains bilingual texts and corresponding images is required to train a MNMT system with image features. However, such a corpus is not available for low resource language pairs. To address this, we developed both a synthetic training dataset and a manually curated development/test dataset for Hindi based on an existing English-image parallel corpus. We used these datasets to build our image description translation system by adopting state-of-the-art MNMT models. Our results show that it is possible to train a MNMT system for low-resource language pairs through the use of synthetic data and that such a system can benefit from image features.

1 Introduction

Recent years have witnessed a surge in application of multimodal neural models as a sequence to sequence learning problem (Sutskever et al., 2014; Kalchbrenner and Blunsom, 2013; Cho et al., 2014b) for solving different tasks such as machine translations (Huang et al., 2016), image and video description generation (Karpathy and Fei-Fei, 2015; Kiros et al., 2014; Donahue et al., 2015; Venugopalan et al., 2014), visual question answering (Antol et al., 2015), etc. However, neural machine translation (NMT), which is an inherently data-dependent procedure, continues to be a challenging problem in the context of low-resourced and out-of-domain settings (Koehn and Knowles, 2017). In other words, there is a concern that the model will perform poorly with languages having limited resources, especially in comparison with well-resourced major languages.

Although English(En) and Hindi(Hi) languages belong to the same family (Indo-European), they differ significantly in terms of word order, syntax and morphological structure (Bharati et al., 1995). While English maintains a Subject-Verb-Object (SVO) template, Hindi follows a Subject-Object-Verb (SOV) convention. Moreover, compared to English, Hindi has a more complex inflection system, where nouns, verbs and adjectives are inflected according to number, gender and case. These issues, combined with the data scarcity problem, makes Hi→En machine translation a challenging task.

Bilingual corpora, which are an important component for machine translation systems, suffer from the problem of data scarcity when one of the languages is resource-poor. To achieve better quality translation, a potential solution is to extend along the language dimension to construct bilingual corpora. In particular, for a distant language pair such as Hindi and English, building a bilingual corpus can prove to be a useful endeavor in multiple aspects.

Proceedings of the Workshop on Deep Learning Approaches for Low-Resource NLP, pages 33–42
Melbourne, Australia July 19, 2018. ©2018 Association for Computational Linguistics

We are inspired by the recent successes of using visual inputs for translation tasks (see Section 2 for relevant studies). For translating image descriptions, given both the source image and it's description, it can be seen that both modalities can bring more useful information for generating the target language description. With the goal of preventing a low-resource language such as Hindi from being left behind in the advancement of multimodal machine translation, we take the first steps towards applying MNMT methods for Hi→En translation.

Our contributions in this study are as follows:

- To the best of our knowledge, we are the first to tackle the problem of multimodal translation from Hindi into English.

- We examine if visual features help to improve machine translation (MT) performance in low resource scenarios.

- We investigate whether the multimodal machine translation system for less-resourced language can benefit from synthetic data.

- We augment the Flickr30k dataset with synthetic Hindi descriptions, obtained from a MT system.

- We manually develop a validation and test corpus of the English counterpart in the Flickr30k dataset. We plan to release this dataset publicly for research purposes.

This paper is divided as follows: Section 2 provides the necessary background and establishes the relevance of the presented work, both in terms of low-resourced MT and MT in multimodal contexts. Section 3 describes the overall methodology. In Section 4 we outline the backgrounds of datasets used for training, validation and testing. Section 5 provides detailed descriptions of the multimodal models used in our experiments. Section 6 details the experimental set-ups. Results and analysis are presented in Section 7. Finally, in Section 8, we provide conclusions and indicate possible directions for future work.

2   Related Work

There has been some previous work on using visual context in tasks involving both neural machine translation (NMT) and image description generation (IDG) that explicitly uses an encoder-decoder framework as an instantiation of the sequence to sequence (seq2seq) learning problem (Cho et al., 2014a). Vinyals et al. (2015) proposed an IDG model that uses a vector, encoding the image as input based on the sequence-to-sequence framework. Specia et al. (2016) introduced a shared task to investigate the role of images in Multi-modal MT. Similarly, Huang et al. (2016) introduced a model to associate textual and visual features extracted with the VGG19 network for translation tasks (Simonyan and Zisserman, 2014). Elliott et al. (2015) generated multilingual image descriptions using image features transferred from separate non-attentive neural image description models. Calixto et al. (2017a) carried out experiments to incorporate spatial visual information into NMT using a separate visual attention mechanism. Although these approaches have demonstrated the plausibility of multilingual natural language processing with multiple modalities, they rely exclusively on the availability of a large three-way parallel corpus (bilingual captions corresponding to the image) as training data.

Having enough parallel corpora is a big challenge in NMT and it is very unlikely to have millions of parallel sentences for every language pair. Therefore, quite a few attempts have been made to build NMT systems for low-resource language pairs (Sennrich et al., 2016; Zhang and Zong, 2016) which focused on building NMT systems in a low-resource scenario. They incorporated huge monolingual corpus in the source or target side. Gulcehre et al. (2017) proposed two alternative methods to integrate monolingual data on target side, namely shallow fusion and deep fusion. In shallow fusion, the top K hypotheses (produced by NMT) at each time step t are re-scored using the weighted sum of the scores given by the NMT(trained on parallel data) and a recurrent neural network based language model (RNNLM). Whereas in deep fusion, hidden states obtained at each time step t of RNNLM and NMT are concatenated and output is generated from that concatenated state.

Sennrich et al. (2016) incorporated monolingual data on the target side to investigate two methods of filling the source side of the monolingual data. In the first method, they used a dummy source sentence for every target sentence, while in the second method synthetic source sentences were obtained via back-translation. Their results found that the second method is more effective. In a similar vein, Zhang and Zong (2016) explored the effect of incorporating large-scale source-side monolingual in NMT in many ways. In the first approach, inspired by Sennrich et al. (2016), they built a baseline system and then obtained parallel synthetic data by translating the monolingual data. This parallel data, along with the original data, is used again for training an attention-based encoder-decoder NMT system. Their second method involved the multi-task learning framework to generate the target translation and the reordered source-side sentences at the same time. They discovered that the use of source-side monolingual data in NMT is more effective than in SMT.

A few other popular approaches in this area involve using a method called transfer learning which focuses on sharing parameters, such as source side word-embeddings across related language pairs. Zoph et al. (2016) focus on training a model on high resource language pair and then using learned parameters to train the low resource language pair. However, it requires selecting closely related high and low resource language pairs. So this approach might not work if the language pairs are distant.

Most of the previous related work on this problem of low-resource NMT has tried to incorporate monolingual data in source or target side. The effect of adding monolingual data in NMT is similar to that of building language model (LM) on large-scale monolingual data in SMT. While in SMT it can make the output more fluent, adding monolingual data does not contribute much in improving adequacy for NMT.

3 Methodology Overview

We formulate the task of augmenting the Flickr30k dataset with Hindi descriptions as a multimodal NMT task. The task is defined as follows.

To produce a target side description of an image i in Flickr30k dataset, a MT system may use unimodal information such as text in the form of description for image i in the source language En, as well as multimodal information such as text plus visual features embedded in the image i itself. Our overall approach consists of the following steps.

- Due to the unavailability of in-domain Hindi-English parallel corpus for our caption translation task, we use a general domain Hindi-English parallel corpus (referred as $Hi_c - En_c$ hereafter) which is compiled from a variety of existing sources. Details of the dataset are described in Section 4.

- Building a phrase based statistical machine translation(PBSMT) system using $Hi_c - En_c$ parallel corpus. To create a synthetic in-domain Hindi-English parallel corpus for the image descriptions translation task, we translate the English descriptions of Flickr30k dataset (referred to as E_n (Manl.Trans.)) into Hindi, using a PBSMT system. We take motivation for using the PBSMT system over NMT from the work carried out by Kunchukuttan et al. (2017). For $Hi \rightarrow En$ translation, their system achieves better results with PBSMT over NMT when trained on the same corpus.

- We divide the E_n (Manl.Trans.) into training, validation and test set and call these as En_t (Manl.Train.Trans.), En_d (Manl.Dev.Trans.) and En_r (Manl.Test.Trans.), respectively. We translate the En_t (Manl.Train.Trans) into Hindi using the PBSMT system and call these as Hi_t (Syn.Train.Trans).We manually translate En_d (Manl.Dev.Trans) and En_r (Manl.Test.Trans) into Hindi. We refer to these manually translated English descriptions as Hi_d (Manl.Dev.Trans) and Hi_r (Manl.Test.Trans).

- We use synthetic training data to build a text-only baseline NMT system. In particular we use En_t (Manl.Train.Trans) and its automatically translated Hindi counter part Hi_t (Syn.Train.Trans) to train the system. In addition to this, we use Hi_d (Manl.Dev.Trans.) and En_d (Manl.Dev.Trans.) to tune the system.

- Visual input may provide right-angled information that is free of the natural language ambiguities and can serve as extraneous information to textual features for machine translation in multimodal scenarios. This motivates us to extract deep visual semantic features from the entire image. We use a pre-trained-convolutional neural network(CNN) model to extract visual global features for all the images in Flickr30k dataset.

- We build MNMT system using the En_t (Manl.Train.Trans.)-Hi_t (Syn.Train.Trans.) parallel corpus and the extracted visual features. We use Hi_d (Manl.Dev.Trans.) and En_d (Manl.Dev.Trans.) to tune the system.

- Finally, we translate Hi_r (Manl.Test.Trans.) into English and measure the performance with reference to En_r (Manl.Test.Trans.)

4 Data

$\underline{\textbf{Hi}_\textbf{c} - \textbf{En}_\textbf{c}}$: In order to generate the synthetic data by means of back-translation, we use the general domain IITB English-Hindi Corpus to train a PBSMT system. The corpus is a compilation of parallel corpora collected from a various existing sources such as OPUS (Tiedemann, 2012), HindEn (Bojar et al., 2014b) and TED (Abdelali et al., 2014) as well as corpora developed at the Center for Indian Language Technology, IIT-B [1] over the years (Kunchukuttan et al., 2017).

$\underline{\textbf{Hi}_\textbf{t}(\textbf{Syn.Trans})}$: We divide the English descriptions of Flickr30k dataset consisting of 158,915 sentences into training, development and test sets. The training dataset $(En_t(Manl.Trans))$ contains

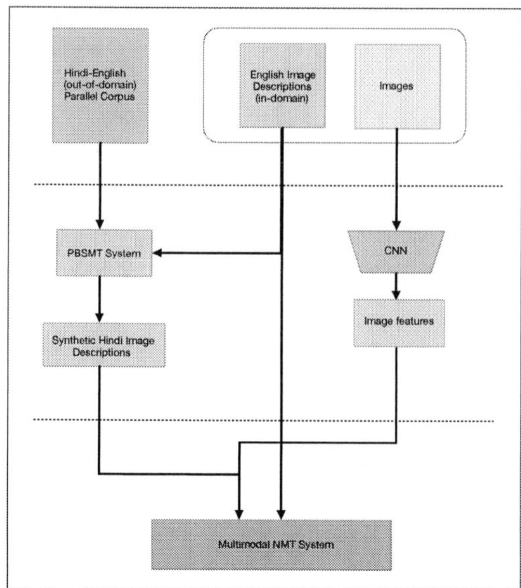

Figure 1: Architecture of the Hi-En MNMT System.

156,915 sentences, the development dataset $(En_d(Manl.Trans))$ contains 1,000 sentences and the test set $(En_r(Manl.Trans))$ contains 1000 sentences. We use the PBSMT system trained on $Hi_c - En_c$ to translate the $En_t(Manl.Trans)$ set into Hindi by means of back-translation. Such a strategy represents the case where there is no parallel resources available but domain-specific monolingual data can be translated via an existing MT system and further provided as a training corpus to a new MT system. $\textbf{Hi}_\textbf{d}(\textbf{Manl.Trans})$ and $\textbf{Hi}_\textbf{r}(\textbf{Manl.Trans})$: for manually curating the dataset, we were assisted by two bilingual speakers of Hindi and English. One of them translated the datasets $En_d(Manl.Trans)$ and $En_r(ManlTrans)$ into Hindi while the other speaker verified the same.

The examples of manually translated descriptions are shown in Table 4.

Data	#Sentences	#Tokens	
		En	Hi
Train	1,492,827	20,667,259	22,171,543
Dev	3207	68459	74027

Table 1: Statistics of data sets used to train PBSMT system

Data–set	#sentences
Monolingual	45,075,279

Table 2: Additional monolingual (Hi) text used for training the language model to create synthetic Hindi data

Data–set	#sentences
Monolingual	20,638,520

Table 3: Additional monolingual (En) text used for training the general domain PBSMT system

5 Multimodal NMT Architecture

In our experiments, we use models which can essentially be thought of as extensions of the attentive NMT framework of Bahdanau et al. (2015). However, following Calixto et al. (2017b) we have included an additional visual component for incorporating the visual features from images. For the encoder, we use a bi-directional recurrent neural network (RNN) with gated recurrent unit (GRU) (Cho et al., 2014a), while the concatenation of forward and backward hidden states, $h_i = [\overrightarrow{h_i}, \overleftarrow{h_i}]$ serves as the final annotation vector for a given source position i. In subsections 5.2 and 5.3 we describe the two multi-modal NMT models used in our experiments. For a detailed description of these models, we refer the reader to Calixto et al. (2017b).

5.1 Image feature extraction

For all the images, the global image feature vectors, which are the 4096D activations of the penultimate fully connected layer FC7, (henceforth referred to as $\mathbf{q}$), are extracted using a publicly available pre-trained model VGG19-CNN (Simonyan and Zisserman, 2014) which is trained for classifying images into one out of 1000 Imagenet classes (Russakovsky et al., 2015). In our experiment, we pass all images in our dataset through the pre-trained 19-layers VGG network (VGG19-CNN) to extract global image features and incorporate them - (i) to initialise the encoder hidden state and (ii) as additional input to initialise the decoder hidden state.

English Source Sentence	Hindi Translation *(Manual)*
A man in an orange hat starring at something .	एक नारंगी टोपी में एक आदमी घूर रहा है ।
People are fixing the roof of a house .	लोग एक घर की छत ठीक कर रहे हैं ।
Group of Asian boys wait for meat to cook over barbecue .	एशियाई लड़कों का समूह बारबेक्यू पर खाना बनाने के लिए मांस का इंतजार करता है ।
The person in the striped shirt is mountain climbing .	धारीदार शर्ट में व्यक्ति पहाड़ चढ़ाई कर रहा ।

Table 4: Examples of manual curated captions of the Flickr30k English descriptions in Hindi using PBSMT system. First column represents the original English captions. Second column represents the manually curated English captions in Hindi.

5.2 IMG$_\mathrm{E}$: Image for encoder initialization

Instead of initializing the hidden state of the encoder with the zero vector $\overrightarrow{0}$, as in the original attention-based NMT model of Bahdanau et al. (2015) we use two new single-layer feed-forward neural networks to compute the initial states of the forward and backward RNN, respectively.

We use Equation (1) to compute a vector $\mathbf{d}$ from the global image feature vector $\mathbf{q} \in \mathbb{R}^{4096}$:

$$\mathbf{d} = \mathbf{W}_I^2.(\mathbf{W}_I^1.\mathbf{q} + \mathbf{b}_I^1) + \mathbf{b}_I^2. \qquad (1)$$

Here $\mathbf{W}$ and $\mathbf{b}$ denote the projection matrix and bias vector, respectively, such that $\mathbf{W}_I^1 \in \mathbb{R}^{4096 \times 4096}$ and $\mathbf{b}_I^1 \in \mathbb{R}^{4096}$ while $\mathbf{W}_I^2$ and $\mathbf{b}_I^2$ project the image features into the same dimensionality as the hidden states of the source language encoder.

The encoder hidden state is initialized by the feed-forward networks computed as follows:

$$\overleftarrow{h}_{\mathrm{init}} = \tanh(\mathbf{W}_f \mathbf{d} + \mathbf{b}_f),$$
$$\overrightarrow{h}_{\mathrm{init}} = \tanh(\mathbf{W}_b \mathbf{d} + \mathbf{b}_b), \qquad (2)$$

where $\mathbf{b}$ and $\mathbf{W}$ are respectively the bias vector and the multi-modal projection matrix for projecting the image features $\mathbf{d}$ into the encoder hidden state's dimensionality. The suffix 'f' ('b') corresponds to forward (backward) states.

5.3 IMG$_D$: Image for decoder initialization

A new single-layer feed-forward neural network is used for incorporating an image into the decoder. Originally, the initial hidden state of the decoder is computed from the encoder's hidden states, often from concatenation of the last hidden states of the encoder forward RNN and backward RNN, respectively $\overrightarrow{h}_N$ and $\overleftarrow{h}_1$, or from the mean of the source-language annotation vectors h_i. However, here we compute the initial hidden state $\mathbf{s}_0$ of the decoder by including the image features as additional inputs as follows:

$$\mathbf{s}_0 = \tanh(\mathbf{W}_{di}[\overleftarrow{\mathbf{h}}_1; \overrightarrow{\mathbf{h}}_N]) + \mathbf{W}_m\mathbf{d} + \mathbf{b}_{di}, \quad (3)$$

where $\mathbf{W}_{di}$ and $\mathbf{b}_{di}$ are learned model parameters while the image feature $\mathbf{d}$ is projected into the decoder hidden state dimensionality by the multi-modal projection matrix $\mathbf{W}_m$.

As before, given the global image vector $\mathbf{q} \in \mathbb{R}^{4096}$, the vector $\mathbf{d}$ is calculated from Equation (1). However, in the present case, the image features are projected into the same dimensionality as the decoder hidden states by the parameters $\mathbf{W}_I^2$ and $\mathbf{b}_I^2$.

6 Experiment Set–Up

In this section, we briefly describe the experimental settings used to generate the synthetic Hindi data and further expand it into a multi-modal NMT framework.

The Hindi side of the $Hi_c - En_c$ is normalized using the Indic_NLP_Library[2] to ensure the canonical Unicode representation. We used the scripts from the above library to tokenize and normalize the Hindi sentences. For English, we used the scripts from the Moses tokenizer *tokenizer.perl*[3] to tokenize and lowercase the English representations for our experiments. We use settings similar to that of (Kunchukuttan et al., 2017) to develop Hi_t. They used the news stories from the WMT 2014 English-Hindi shared task (Bojar et al., 2014a) as the development(dev) and test corpora which we concatenate together to create our dev set. The training and dev corpora consist of 1,492,827 and 3,207 sentence segments respectively. We used the HindMono corpus (Bojar et al., 2014b) which contains roughly 45 million sentences to build our language model in Hindi. The corpus statistics are shown in Table.1 and Table.2. For training the $Hi_c - En_c$ corpus, we use the Moses SMT system (Koehn et al., 2007) . We use the SRILM toolkit (Stolcke, 2002) for building a language model and GIZA++ (Och and Ney, 2000) with the grow-diag-final-and heuristic for extracting phrases from $Hi_c - En_c$ .The trained system is tuned using Minimum Error Rate Training (Och, 2003). For other parameters of Moses, default values are used. If the sentences in English or Hindi are longer than 80 tokens, they are discarded. To measure the performance of the system, we also translate the En_r testset into Hi_r both manually and automatically.

We also perform Hindi→English (Hi→En) translation using a PBSMT system with the general domain $Hi_c - En_c$ corpus. We use the News Crawl articles 2016 from the WMT17 [4] as additional English monolingual corpora to train the 4-gram language model. This contain roughly 20 million sentence for English. (Table 3).

To build our Multi-modal NMT systems we use OpenNMT-py (the pytorch port of OpenNMT (Klein et al., 2017)) following the settings of Calixto et al. (2017b) which implements the encoder as a bi-directional RNN with GRU, one 1024D single-layer forward RNN and one 1024D single-layer backward RNN. Throughout the experiments, the models are parameterised using 620D source and target word embeddings, and both are trained jointly with the model. All non-recurrent matrices are initialised by sampling from a Gaussian distribution ($\mu = 0, \sigma = 0.01$), re-

---

[2]https://bitbucket.org/anoopk/indic_nlp_library

[3]https://github.com/moses-smt/mosesdecoder/blob/RELEASE-3.0/scripts/tokenizer/tokenizer.perl

[4]http://www.statmt.org/wmt17/translation-task.html

current matrices are random orthogonal and bias vectors are all initialised to 0. Dropout with a probability of 0.3 in source and target word embeddings, in the image features (in all MNMT models), in the encoder and decoder RNNs inputs and recurrent connections, and before the readout operation in the decoder RNN was applied. Following (Gal and Ghahramani, 2016), dropout to the encoder bidirectional RNN and decoder RNN using the same mask in all time steps are also applied. The models are trained for 25 epochs using Adam (Kingma and Ba, 2015) with learning rate 0.002 and mini-batches of size 40, where each training instance consists of one English sentence, one Hindi sentence and one image.

Finally, we evaluate translation quality quantitatively in terms of BLEU (Papineni et al., 2002) and METEOR (Denkowski and Lavie, 2014) and report statistical significance for the metrics using approximate randomisation computed with MultEval (Clark et al., 2011).

7 Results and Analysis

7.1 Quantitative Analysis

We develop the following five systems -

- **PBSMT**$_{out}$: a phrase based machine translation system trained on the general-domain $\mathbf{Hi_c - En_c}$ corpus.

- **PBSMT**$_{In}$: a phrase based machine translation system trained on the in-domain $\mathbf{Hi_{it} - En_{it}}$ corpus.

- **NMT**$_{text}$: a text-only NMT system trained on the in-domain $\mathbf{Hi_{it} - En_{it}}$ corpus.

- **IMG**$_D$: the multimodal machine system that uses images as an additional input at the decoding stage.

- **IMG**$_E$: the multimodal machine system that uses images to initialise the encoder hidden state.

The comparative evaluation results of our systems are presented in Table 5.

Evaluation is performed against the English translations of the test set using standard MT evaluation metrics, with BLEU and METEOR (multeval implementation, but with METEOR 1.5).

Hi → En	BLEU	METEOR
PBSMT$_{out}$	21.6	29.6
PBSMT$_{in}$	22.7	30.2
NMT$_{text}$	23.3	29.7
IMG$_D$	**24.2**(↑ 0.9)	**30.7**(↑ 1)
IMG$_E$	23.9	29.9

Table 5: Evaluation metrics scores Hi-En translation systems before and after applying the image features on manually curated dev data. Bold numbers indicate that improvements are statistically significant compared to **NMT**$_{text}$ with p = 0.05

Figure 2: Example from the Flickr30k dataset

We see from the results that the text-only NMT model outperforms phrase based SMT model in terms of BLEU score. Our results indicate that incorporating image features in multimodal models helps, as compared to our text-only SMT and NMT baselines. This is reflected in the fact that both the image models are shown to produce better results in terms of BLEU scores with respect to both the SMT and NMT text-only counterpart.

Although IMG$_E$ yields only little improvement over the text-only NMT counterpart, IMG$_D$ performs consistently better in terms of both metrics (BLEU by ↑ 0.9) and (METEOR by ↑ 1) than the strong text-only NMT and SMT baseline.

7.2 Qualitative Analysis

In order to gain a qualitative insight into specific differences between the text-only and image NMT models, we highlight some instances as follows:

English reference: two people wearing odd alien-like costumes , one blue and one purple , are standing in a road .

Manual Source: तदो लोग अजीब विदेशी जैसी वेशभूषा पहनने, एक नीले और एक बैंगनी, एक सड़क में खड़े हैं।

NMT: two people dressed in exotic costumes wear a blue and one flag in a blue , are standing in a road .

MNMT: two people wearing funny foreign attire, one blue and one purple , are standing in a street .

In the first entry, although the NMT system without images incorrectly translated the color 'purple' (as can be seen from Figure. 2, where the costumes are clearly in two colors) the multi-modal model translated it correctly, yielding an improvement in the sentence-level BLEU ($\uparrow$ **21.47**) score. In terms of translations, we see that both the models extrapolate the reference and translate "alien-like costumes" into "exotic costumes" (text-only model) and as a "funny foreign attire" (multimodal model). We attribute this to the fact that the training set is small and contains different forms of biases and unwarranted inferences (van Miltenburg, 2016).

English reference: two young children are on sand.

Manual Source: दो छोटे बच्चे रेत पर हैं।

NMT: two little kids are on the sand.

MNMT: two small children are on sand.

For this particular example, the overall meaning of the source description has been correctly preserved into the target side description for the outputs generated by both models. However, if we closely look into each of the example, we note the difference in entity and its associated attribute. For example, the word-choice for the entity *children* in reference source changes to the term *kids* for text-only NMT but remains intact for MNMT model. Similar trend is observed for the attribute of the entity where the *young* in the reference source is replaced with *little* and *small* for the text and image models respectively. Although every target side entity-attribute pair is semantically close to the source side entity-attribute pair-they may vary in terms of their

usage in conventional English language. Compared to the terminology obtained without the help of the image (*little-kids-* 1417), the one obtained with the help of image (*small children-*1595) tends to be more widely used in standard spoken English according to the 'Corpus of Contemporary American English' [5].

The above examples clearly asserts the positive impact of multimodal models in translation both in quantitative and qualitative sense.

8 Conclusion and Future Work

We presented the results of using synthetic Hindi descriptions of Flickr30k dataset generated via back-translation for multimodal machine translation and provided benchmark baseline results on this corpus.

Our study shows that despite being trained on the same in-domain En–Hi training data, there are inconsistencies in translation quality between the SMT and NMT system, at least in terms of evaluation metrics. These results are not necessarily surprising given that the grammatical syntax between the two languages is poorly represented in the synthetic Hindi training data. In addition to this, Hindi as a language presents many of the well-known issues that NMT currently struggles with (resource sparsity, rich morphology and complex inflection structure). An approach worth considering to address the divergence in word order of the En-Hi language pair is the pre-reordering approach such as the one taken by Ramanathan et al. (2008) to build stronger baseline systems. We will also investigate if incorporating local, spatial-preserving image features can provide more cues to an NMT model as an extension of this work.

In future, we will conduct a more structured study to extend this approach to different language pairs and data scenarios. In addition, we plan to include human evaluation rigorously in our studies to confirm that the MT systems are extended to enhance the translation quality and not simply be tuned to automatic evaluation metrics.

---

[5]https://corpus.byu.edu/coca/

Acknowledgments

This research is supported by Science Foundation Ireland in the ADAPT Centre for Digital Content Technology. The ADAPT Centre for Digital Content Technology is founded under the SFI Research Centres Programme (Grant 13/RC/2106) and is co-funded under the European Regional Development Fund. The authors would like to thank Longyue Wang and Meghan Dowling for providing many good suggestions of improvements, as well as our anonymous reviewers for their valuable comments and feedback.

References

Abdelali, A., Guzman, F., Sajjad, H., and Vogel, S. (2014). The amara corpus: Building parallel language resources for the educational domain. In *LREC*, volume 14, pages 1044–1054.

Antol, S., Agrawal, A., Lu, J., Mitchell, M., Batra, D., Lawrence Zitnick, C., and Parikh, D. (2015). Vqa: Visual question answering. In *Proceedings of the IEEE International Conference on Computer Vision*, pages 2425–2433.

Bahdanau, D., Cho, K., and Bengio, Y. (2015). Neural Machine Translation by Jointly Learning to Align and Translate. In *International Conference on Learning Representations, ICLR 2015*, San Diego, California.

Bharati, A., Chaitanya, V., Sangal, R., and Ramakrishnamacharyulu, K. (1995). *Natural language processing: a Paninian perspective*. Prentice-Hall of India New Delhi.

Bojar, O., Buck, C., Federmann, C., Haddow, B., Koehn, P., Leveling, J., Monz, C., Pecina, P., Post, M., Saint-Amand, H., et al. (2014a). Findings of the 2014 workshop on statistical machine translation. In *Proceedings of the ninth workshop on statistical machine translation*, pages 12–58.

Bojar, O., Diatka, V., Rychlỳ, P., Straňák, P., Suchomel, V., Tamchyna, A., and Zeman, D. (2014b). Hindencorp-hindi-english and hindi-only corpus for machine translation. In *LREC*, pages 3550–3555.

Calixto, I., Liu, Q., and Campbell, N. (2017a). Doubly-Attentive Decoder for Multi-modal Neural Machine Translation. In *Proceedings of the 55th Conference of the Association for Computational Linguistics: Volume 1, Long Papers*, Vancouver, Canada (Paper Accepted).

Calixto, I., Liu, Q., and Campbell, N. (2017b). Incorporating global visual features into attention-based neural machine translation. *CoRR*, abs/1701.06521.

Cho, K., van Merrienboer, B., Gulcehre, C., Bahdanau, D., Bougares, F., Schwenk, H., and Bengio, Y. (2014a). Learning Phrase Representations using RNN Encoder–Decoder for Statistical Machine Translation. In *Proceedings of the 2014 Conference on Empirical Methods in Natural Language Processing (EMNLP)*, pages 1724–1734, Doha, Qatar.

Cho, K., Van Merriënboer, B., Gulcehre, C., Bahdanau, D., Bougares, F., Schwenk, H., and Bengio, Y. (2014b). Learning phrase representations using rnn encoder-decoder for statistical machine translation. *arXiv preprint arXiv:1406.1078*.

Clark, J. H., Dyer, C., Lavie, A., and Smith, N. A. (2011). Better hypothesis testing for statistical machine translation: Controlling for optimizer instability. In *Proceedings of the 49th Annual Meeting of the Association for Computational Linguistics: Human Language Technologies: short papers-Volume 2*, pages 176–181. Association for Computational Linguistics.

Denkowski, M. and Lavie, A. (2014). Meteor Universal: Language Specific Translation Evaluation for Any Target Language. In *Proceedings of the EACL 2014 Workshop on Statistical Machine Translation*, Gothenburg, Sweden. The Association for Computer Linguistics.

Donahue, J., Anne Hendricks, L., Guadarrama, S., Rohrbach, M., Venugopalan, S., Saenko, K., and Darrell, T. (2015). Long-term recurrent convolutional networks for visual recognition and description. In *The IEEE Conference on Computer Vision and Pattern Recognition (CVPR)*.

Elliott, D., Frank, S., and Hasler, E. (2015). Multilingual image description with neural sequence models. *arXiv preprint arXiv:1510.04709*.

Gal, Y. and Ghahramani, Z. (2016). A Theoretically Grounded Application of Dropout in Recurrent Neural Networks. In *Advances in Neural Information Processing Systems, NIPS*, pages 1019–1027, Barcelona, Spain.

Gulcehre, C., Firat, O., Xu, K., Cho, K., and Bengio, Y. (2017). On integrating a language model into neural machine translation. *Computer Speech & Language*, 45:137–148.

Huang, P.-Y., Liu, F., Shiang, S.-R., Oh, J., and Dyer, C. (2016). Attention-based multimodal neural machine translation. In *Proceedings of the First Conference on Machine Translation: Volume 2, Shared Task Papers*, volume 2, pages 639–645.

Kalchbrenner, N. and Blunsom, P. (2013). Recurrent continuous translation models. In *Proceedings of the 2013 Conference on Empirical Methods in Natural Language Processing*, pages 1700–1709.

Karpathy, A. and Fei-Fei, L. (2015). Deep visual-semantic alignments for generating image descriptions. In *The IEEE Conference on Computer Vision and Pattern Recognition (CVPR)*.

Kingma, D. P. and Ba, J. (2015). Adam: A method for stochastic optimization. *International Conference on Learning Representation(ICLR)*.

Kiros, R., Salakhutdinov, R., and Zemel, R. S. (2014). Unifying visual-semantic embeddings with multimodal neural language models. *arXiv preprint arXiv:1411.2539*.

Klein, G., Kim, Y., Deng, Y., Senellart, J., and Rush, A. M. (2017). Opennmt: Open-source toolkit for neural machine translation. *arXiv preprint arXiv:1701.02810*.

Koehn, P., Hoang, H., Birch, A., Callison-Burch, C., Federico, M., Bertoldi, N., Cowan, B., Shen, W., Moran, C., Zens, R., et al. (2007). Moses: Open source toolkit for statistical machine translation. In *Proceedings of the 45th annual meeting of the ACL on interactive poster and demonstration sessions*, pages 177–180. Association for Computational Linguistics.

Koehn, P. and Knowles, R. (2017). Six challenges for neural machine translation. *arXiv preprint arXiv:1706.03872*.

Kunchukuttan, A., Mehta, P., and Bhattacharyya, P. (2017). The iit bombay english-hindi parallel corpus. *arXiv preprint arXiv:1710.02855*.

Och, F. J. (2003). Minimum error rate training in statistical machine translation. In *Proceedings of the 41st Annual Meeting on Association for Computational Linguistics-Volume 1*, pages 160–167. Association for Computational Linguistics.

Och, F. J. and Ney, H. (2000). Giza++: Training of statistical translation models.

Papineni, K., Roukos, S., Ward, T., and Zhu, W.-J. (2002). BLEU: a Method for Automatic Evaluation of Machine Translation. In *Proceedings of the 40th annual meeting on association for computational linguistics*, pages 311–318, Philadelphia, Pennsylvania.

Ramanathan, A., Hegde, J., Shah, R. M., Bhattacharyya, P., and Sasikumar, M. (2008). Simple syntactic and morphological processing can help english-hindi statistical machine translation. In *Proceedings of the Third International Joint Conference on Natural Language Processing: Volume-I*.

Russakovsky, O., Deng, J., Su, H., Krause, J., Satheesh, S., Ma, S., Huang, Z., Karpathy, A., Khosla, A., Bernstein, M., et al. (2015). Imagenet large scale visual recognition challenge. *International Journal of Computer Vision*, 115(3):211–252.

Sennrich, R., Haddow, B., and Birch, A. (2016). Improving neural machine translation models with monolingual data. In *Proceedings of the 54th Annual Meeting of the Association for Computational Linguistics, ACL 2016, August 7-12, 2016, Berlin, Germany*.

Simonyan, K. and Zisserman, A. (2014). Very deep convolutional networks for large-scale image recognition. *arXiv preprint arXiv:1409.1556*.

Specia, L., Frank, S., Sima'an, K., and Elliott, D. (2016). A shared task on multimodal machine translation and crosslingual image description. In *Proceedings of the First Conference on Machine Translation: Volume 2, Shared Task Papers*, volume 2, pages 543–553.

Stolcke, A. (2002). Srilm-an extensible language modeling toolkit. In *Seventh international conference on spoken language processing*.

Sutskever, I., Vinyals, O., and Le, Q. V. (2014). Sequence to sequence learning with neural networks. In *Advances in neural information processing systems*, pages 3104–3112.

Tiedemann, J. (2012). Parallel data, tools and interfaces in opus. In *LREC*, volume 2012, pages 2214–2218.

van Miltenburg, E. (2016). Stereotyping and bias in the flickr30k dataset. *arXiv preprint arXiv:1605.06083*.

Venugopalan, S., Xu, H., Donahue, J., Rohrbach, M., Mooney, R., and Saenko, K. (2014). Translating videos to natural language using deep recurrent neural networks. *arXiv preprint arXiv:1412.4729*.

Vinyals, O., Toshev, A., Bengio, S., and Erhan, D. (2015). Show and tell: A neural image caption generator. In *Computer Vision and Pattern Recognition (CVPR), 2015 IEEE Conference on*, pages 3156–3164. IEEE.

Zhang, J. and Zong, C. (2016). Exploiting source-side monolingual data in neural machine translation. In *Proceedings of the 2016 Conference on Empirical Methods in Natural Language Processing*, pages 1535–1545.

Zoph, B., Yuret, D., May, J., and Knight, K. (2016). Transfer learning for low-resource neural machine translation. pages 1568–1575.

Multi-Task Active Learning for Neural Semantic Role Labeling on Low Resource Conversational Corpus

Fariz Ikhwantri[1]   Samuel Louvan[1,2]   Kemal Kurniawan[1]   Bagas Abisena[1]
Valdi Rachman[3]   Alfan Farizki Wicaksono[3]   Rahmad Mahendra[3]
[1]Kata.ai, Jakarta, Indonesia
[2]Fondazione Bruno Kessler/University of Trento, Trento, Italy
[3]Universitas Indonesia, Depok, Indonesia
{fariz,kemal,bagas}@kata.ai, slouvan@fbk.eu
valdi.rachman@gmail.com
{alfan,rahmad.mahendra}@cs.ui.ac.id

Abstract

Most Semantic Role Labeling (SRL) approaches are supervised methods which require a significant amount of annotated corpus, and the annotation requires linguistic expertise. In this paper, we propose a Multi-Task Active Learning framework for Semantic Role Labeling with Entity Recognition (ER) as the auxiliary task to alleviate the need for extensive data and use additional information from ER to help SRL. We evaluate our approach on Indonesian conversational dataset. Our experiments show that multi-task active learning can outperform single-task active learning method and standard multi-task learning. According to our results, active learning is more efficient by using 12% less of training data compared to passive learning in both single-task and multi-task setting. We also introduce a new dataset for SRL in Indonesian conversational domain to encourage further research in this area[1].

1 Introduction

Semantic Role Labeling (SRL) extracts predicate-argument structures from sentences (Jurafsky and Martin, 2006). It tries to recover information beyond syntax. In particular, information that can answer the question about who did what to whom, when, why and so on (Johansson and Nugues, 2008; Choi et al., 2010).

There have been many proposed SRL techniques, and the high performing models are mostly supervised (Akbik and Li, 2016; Punyakanok et al., 2004). As they are supervised methods, the models are trained on a relatively large annotated corpus. Building such corpus is expensive as it is laborious, time-consuming, and usually requires expertise in linguistics. For example, PropBank annotation guideline by Choi et al. (2010) is around 90 pages so it can be a steep learning curve even for annotators with a linguistic background. This difficulty makes reproducibility hard for creating annotated data especially in low resource language or different domain of data. Several approaches have been proposed to reduce the effort of annotation. He et al. (2015) introduced a Question Answering-driven approach by casting a predicate as a question and its thematic role as an answer in the system. Wang et al. (2017b) used active learning using semantic embedding. Wang et al. (2017a) utilized Annotation Projection with hybrid crowd-sourcing to route between hard instances for linguistic experts and easy instances for non-expert crowds.

Active Learning is the most common method to reduce annotation by using a model to minimize the amount of data to be annotated while maximizing its performance. In this paper, we propose to combine active learning with multi-task learning applied to Semantic Role Labeling by using a related linguistic task as an auxiliary task in an end-to-end role labeling. Our motivation to use a multi-task method is in the same spirit as (Gormley et al., 2014) where they employed related syntactic tasks to improve SRL in low-resource languages as multi-task learning. Instead, we used Entity Recognition (ER) as the auxiliary task because we think ER is semantically related with SRL in some ways. For example, given a sentence: *Andy gives a book to John*, in SRL context, *Andy* and *John* are labeled as AGENT and PATIENT or BENEFACTOR respectively, but in ER context, they are labeled as PERSON. Hence, although the labels are different, we hypothesize

---

[1] request to research@kata.ai

Proceedings of the Workshop on Deep Learning Approaches for Low-Resource NLP, pages 43–50
Melbourne, Australia July 19, 2018. ©2018 Association for Computational Linguistics

that there is some useful information from ER that can be leveraged to improve overall SRL performance.

Our contribution in this paper consists of two parts. First, we propose to train multi-task active learning with Semantic Role Labeling as the primary task and Entity Recognition as the auxiliary task. Second, we introduce a new dataset and annotation tags for Semantic Role Labeling from conversational chat logs between a bot and human users. While many of the previous work studied SRL on large scale English datasets in news domain, our research aims to explore SRL in Indonesian conversational language, which is still under-resourced.

2 Related Work

Active learning (AL) (Settles, 2012) is a method to improve the performance of a learner by iteratively asking a new set of hypotheses to be labeled by human experts. A well-known method is Pool-Based AL, which selects the hypotheses predicted from a pool of unlabeled data (Lewis and Gale, 1994). The most informative instance from hypotheses is selected and added into labeled data. The informativeness of an instance is measured by its uncertainty, which is inversely proportional to the learner's confidence of its prediction for that instance. In other words, the most informative instance is the one which the model is least confident with.

There are two well-studied methods of sequence labeling with active learning. The first one is maximum entropy: given an input sentence x, the probability of word x_t having tag y_t is given by

$$p_\theta(y_t|x_t) = \frac{exp(\ a_t^{y_t}(x_t|\theta))}{\sum_{j=1}^{K} exp(\ a_t^{j}(x_t|\theta))} \quad (1)$$

Where θ denotes a model parameters and K is the number of tags. Uncertainty in maximum entropy can be defined using Token Entropy (TE) as described in (Settles and Craven, 2008; Marcheggiani and Artières, 2014).

$$\phi_t^{\text{TE}} = -\sum_{j \in K} p(y_t = j|x_t) \log p(y_t = j|x_t) \quad (2)$$

$$x_{\text{TE}} = \arg\max_x \sum_{t=1}^{T} -\phi_t^{\text{TE}} \quad (3)$$

From token level entropy (TE) in (2), we used a simple aggregation such as summation to select an instance. So that instance x is selected by Equation (3) as least confident sample, where $\sum_{t=1}^{T}(.)$ is a summation term for greedy aggregation of sentence level entropy.

Another well-studied sequence labeling method with active learning is Conditional Random Fields (CRFs) by Lafferty et al. (2001), where the probability of a sequence label $\mathbf{y} = \{y_1, y_2, .., y_T\}$ given a sequence of observed vectors $\mathbf{x} = \{x_1, x_2, .., x_T\}$ and a joint log-likelihood function of unary and transition parameter $\psi(y_{t-1}, y_t, x_t)$ is defined as

$$p_\psi(y|x) = \frac{\prod_{t=1}^{T} \psi(y_{t-1}, y_t, x_t)}{\sum_{y \in Y} \prod_{t=1}^{T} \psi(y_{t-1}, y_t, x_t)} \quad (4)$$

Uncertainty in conditional random fields can be obtained by Viterbi decoding by selecting instance with maximum $p(y|x)$ from a pool of unlabeled instances as defined below.

$$x_{\text{VE}} = \arg\min_x p_\psi(y^\star|x) \quad (5)$$

where $p(y^\star|.)$ is a probability assigned by Viterbi inference algorithm (Marcheggiani and Artières, 2014).

Multi-Task Learning Instead of training one task per model independently, one can use related labels to optimize multiple tasks in a learning process jointly. This method is commonly known as Multi-Task learning (MTL) or as Parallel Transfer Learning (Caruana, 1997). Our motivation to use multi-task learning is to leverage "easier" annotation than Semantic Roles to regularize model by using related tasks. Previous work on Multi-Task learning on Semantic Role Labeling by Collobert et al. (2011) did not report any significant improvement for SRL task. A recent work (Marasovic and Frank, 2017) used SRL as the auxiliary task with Opinion Role Labeling as the main task.

Multi-Task Active Learning Previous work on multi-task active learning (MT-AL) (Reichart et al., 2008) was focused on formulating a method to keep the performance across a set of tasks instead of a single task. In multi-task active learning scenario, optimizing a set of task classifiers can be regarded as a meta-protocol by combining each task query strategy into a single query method. In one-sided task query scenario settings,

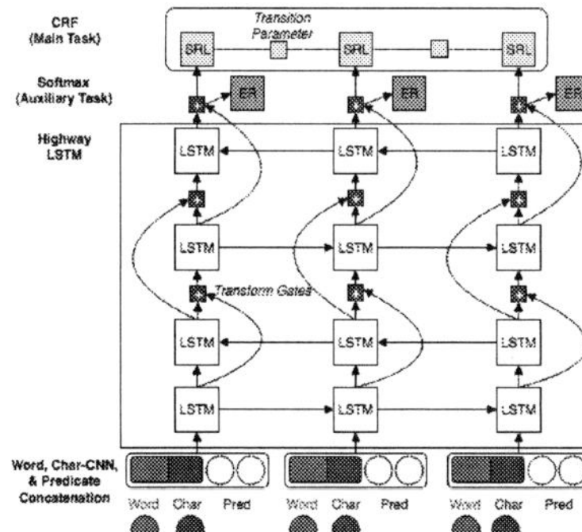

Figure 1: Model Overview. Four layers Highway LSTM. SRL task used Conditional Random Fields (CRF) for sequence labeling output.

one selected task classifier uncertainty strategy is used to query unlabeled samples. In multiple task scenario, the uncertainty of an instance is the aggregate of classifiers uncertainties for all tasks.

3 Proposed Method

In this section, we explain on how we incorporated both the AL and MTL in our neural network architecture. We used the state-of-the-art SRL model from He et al. (2017) as our base model as shown in Figure 1.

Our model is a modification of He et al.'s work. Our first adjustment is to use CRF as the last layer instead of softmax because of its notable superiority found by Reimers and Gurevych (2017) for both role labeling and entity recognition. In this scenario, we used CRF layer for the primary task (SRL) (Zhou and Xu, 2015) and softmax layer for the auxiliary task. The auxiliary task acts as a regularization method (Caruana, 1997). Second, we used character embedding with Convolutional Neural Networks as Characters Encoder (Ma and Hovy, 2016), to handle out-of-vocabulary problem caused by misspelled words, slangs, and abbreviations common in informal chatting, as well as word embedding and predicate indicator feature embedding as the input features for a Highway LSTM.

In multi-task learning configuration, we used parameter sharing in embedding and sequence encoder layers except for the outermost module which is used for prediction for each specific task. We optimized the parameters jointly by minimizing the sum loss of $L(y_s, y_e|x, \theta, \psi) = L(\hat{y_s}, y_s|x, \theta) + L(\hat{y_e}, y_e|x, \psi)$, where the first part

Table 1: Semantic Roles dataset for conversational language statistics and examples

Semantic Roles	Count	Example
AGENT (A)	2843	*I* brought you a present
PATIENT (PS)	3040	I brought you *a present*
BENEFACTOR (BN)	293	I brought *you* a present
GREET (G)	572	Hi *Andy*!
		I brought you a present
LOCATION (L)	183	I can eat at *home* today
TIME (T)	399	I can eat at home *today*

of the equation is the SRL loss and the second part is the entity loss. SRL loss is computed by joint log-likelihood of emissions with transition parameters in CRF from Equation 4 and entity loss is computed using standard cross-entropy loss from softmax output in Equation 1.

Multi-Task Active Learning In multiple task scenario, we used the rank combination by Reichart et al. (2008) that combines each task query strategy into an overall $\text{rank}(x^i) = \text{rank}(x^i_{\text{VE}}) + \text{rank}(x^i_{\text{TE}})$. Note that in both training one-sided and combined rank multi-task active learning, we returned all task gold labels to be trained in multi-task models.

As a multi-task active learning baseline, instead of one-sided AL which queries a pre-determined task for all-iteration, we used random task selection to draw which task to use as the query strategy in the i-th iteration. Random task selection is implemented using random multinomial sampling. The selected task is used for the query instances using standard uncertainty sampling.

4 Dataset & Experiment

4.1 Dataset

This research presents the dataset of human users conversation with virtual friends bot[2]. The annotated messages are user inquiries or responses to the bot. Private information in the original data such as name, email, and address will be anonymized. Three annotators with a linguistic background performed the annotation process. In this work, we used a set of semantic roles adapted for informal, conversational language. Table 1 shows some examples of the semantic roles. The dataset consists of 6057 unique sentences which contain predicates.

---

[2]https://kata.ai/case-studies/jemma

The semantic roles used are a subset of Prop-Bank (Palmer et al., 2005). Also, we added a new role, GREET. In our collected data, Indonesian people tend to call the name of the person they are talking to. Because such case frequently co-occurs with another role, we felt the need to differentiate this previously mentioned entity as a new role. For example, in the following sentence: *Hi Andy! I brought you a present* can help refers *"you"* role as PATIENT to *"Andi"* role as GREET instead of left unassigned.

In our second task, which is Entity Recognition (ER), we annotated the same sentence after the SRL annotation. We used common labels such as PERSON, LOCATION, ORGANIZATION, and MISC as our entity tags. Different from Named Entity Recognition (NER), ER also tag nominal objects such as *"I"*, *"you"* and referential locations like *"di sana (over there)"*. While this tagging might raise a question whether there are overlapping tags with SRL, we argue that entity labels are less ambiguous compared to role arguments which are dependent on the predicate. An example of this case can be seen in Table 1, where both of *I* and *you* are tagged as PERSON whereas the roles are varied. In this task, we used semi-automatic annotation tools using brat (Stenetorp et al., 2012). These annotation were checked and fixed by four people and one linguistic expert.

4.2 Experiment Scenario

The purpose of the experiment is to understand whether multi-task learning and active learning help to improve SRL model performance compared to the baseline model (SRL with no AL scenario). In this section, we focus on several experiment scenarios: single-task SRL, single-task SRL with AL, MTL, and MTL with AL.

Model Architecture Our model architecture consists of word embedding, character 5-gram encoder using CNN and predicate embedding as inputs, with 50, 50, and 100 dimension respectively. These inputs are concatenated into a 200-dimensional vector which then fed into two-layer Highway LSTM with 300 hidden units.

Initialization The word embedding were initialized with unsupervised pre-trained values obtained from training word2vec (Mikolov et al., 2013) on the dataset. Word tokens were lowercased, while characters were not.

	Scenario		Metric		
Task	Active	Data (%)	P	R	F1
SRL	-	100	75.12	75.49	75.30
SRL	Random	50	75.50	74.01	74.75
SRL	Random	85	78.83	71.91	75.21
SRL	Uncertain	50	76.67	74.01	75.32
SRL	Uncertain	85	78.35	75.25	76.77
SRL+ER	-	100	76.88	74.50	75.67
SRL+ER	RandTask	50	77.31	71.28	74.18
SRL+ER	RandTask	85	76.59	74.50	75.53
SRL+ER	Ranking	50	78.94	71.90	75.25
SRL+ER	Ranking	85	78.18	75.87	**77.01**

Table 2: Experiment results, Scenario Active means the query strategy used to sort instance informativeness, RandTask = Random Task Selection, Data scenario are initial percentage of labeled data, 50% means the 50:50 split, 85% means 85:15 split, and 100% means use all training data. P (Precision), R (Recall), F1 (F1 Score)

Training Configurations For training configurations, we trained for 10 epochs using AdaDelta (Zeiler, 2012) with $\rho = 0.95$ and $\epsilon = 1.e-6$. We also employed early stopping with patience set to 3. We split our data using 80% training, 10% validation, and 10% test for the fully supervised scenario. For the active learning scenario, we further split the training data into labeled and unlabeled data. We used two kinds of split, 50:50 and 85:15. For the 50:50 scenario, we queried 100 sentences for each epoch. For the 85:15 scenario, we used a smaller query of 10 sentences in an epoch to keep the number of queries less than the number of available fully supervised training data in 10 epochs. This number of queried sentences was obtained by tuning on the validation set.

As for the AL query method, in the single-task SRL, we used random and uncertainty sampling query. SRL with 100% training data and SRL with random query serve as baseline strategies. In the MTL SRL, we employed random task and ranking.

5 Results & Analysis

We experimented with a low-resource conversational language by varying the task scenario, active learning query strategy, and outset percentage of data seed from training data. We report our results using Precision (P), Recall (R), and the F1 score (F1) computed by exact matching of gold and predicted role spans. The report can be seen

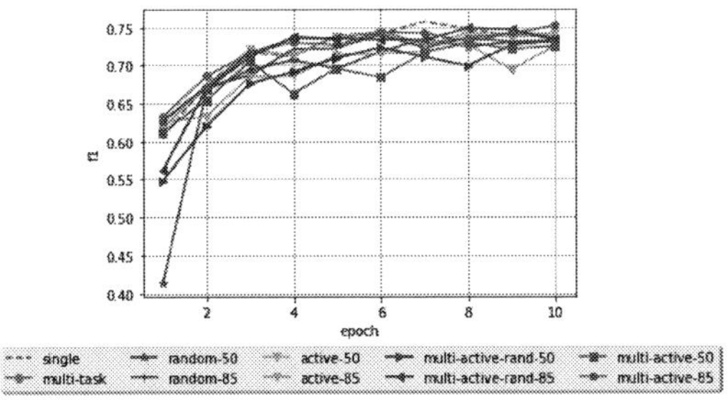

Figure 2: Comparison of experiment scenarios in validation set. Multi-Task AL using Ranking Combination with initial 85% labeled training data achieve best F1 score

Label	dev			test		
	P	R	F1	P	R	F1
AGENT	87.03	83.43	85.196	86.68	85.85	86.26
PATIENT	72.80	69.64	71.19	74.00	70.76	72.34
BENEFACTOR	60.53	76.67	67.65	38.10	42.11	40.00
GREET	75.81	65.28	70.15	83.05	76.56	79.66
LOCATION	50.00	34.62	40.91	60.00	65.22	62.50
TIME	66.67	61.11	63.76	72.73	65.31	68.82

Table 3: Detailed scores of Multi-Task Active Learning performance with 85% initial data. P (Precision), R (Recall), F1 (F1 Score)

in Table 2.

Our baseline multi-task (SRL+ER with no AL scenario) learning model in this experiment has a higher precision compared to the single-task (SRL) model. From the initial 85% of labeled training data scenario, our model in total requested 87% of the training data in 10 epochs. In this scenario, our proposed method for multi-task active learning using ranking combination can outperform the single-task active learning models. Figure 2 presents the F1 score learning curve for each model.

Significance test We performed two tails significance test (t-test) by using 5-fold cross validation from the training and the test parts of the corpus. The multi-task learning model is better compared to the single-task learning one ($p <$ 0.05). However, the single-task and the multi-task learning scenario are not significantly better than both multi-task active learning from 85% and 50% training data scenario, since the p-value between model pairs are greater than 0.05. Therefore, accepting the null hypothesis indicate that performances between multi-task active learning with 50%/85% initial data and multi-task or single-task with full dataset are comparable.

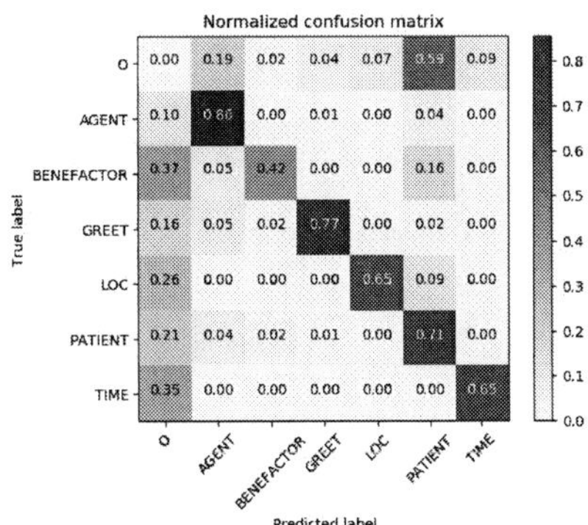

Figure 3: Confusion matrix for Multi-Task Active Learning Model using 85% initial labeled data.

We draw a confusion matrix of the multi-task active learning model with 85% initial training data in Figure 3 to analyze our model performance. We observe several common errors made by the model. The largest mistakes from the matrix are PATIENT false positive. The model incorrectly detected 59% of non-roles as PATIENT. Another prominent error is 21% false negative of total gold roles. The model primarily failed to tag 37% of gold BENEFACTOR and 35% of gold TIME. Quite different from the English SRL, we found that labels confusion happens less frequently than other error types. Based on this percentage, we investigated the error by drawing samples. In general, we broke down the incorrect predictions into several types of error.

False Negative Spans

False negatives in semantic role labeling are defined as the number of roles in the gold data that do not have the corresponding span matches in the model prediction. False negative for AGENT encompasses 69% of errors from the total of 45 AGENT gold span role errors, while the errors in TIME roles all occur in this error type. In Table 4, the left example shows that, the model failed to tag *"ini komputer"* (EN: This is a computer). In the right example, the model did not recognize *"get rick nya*[3]*"* as PATIENT. An interesting remark is perhaps how the model failed to tag because the predicate is an unknown word in the training vocabulary despite the use of characters encoder to alleviate the out-of-vocabulary problem. While in the left example, predicate *"menjawab"* is also an unknown word in the vocabulary

---

[3]mistyped application name

Predicate : *menjawab* (EN: reply)

token	vocab	gold	predicted
Yang	Yang	O	O
menjawab	UNK	O	O
ini	ini	B-PS	O
komputer	komputer	I-PS	O
kan	kan	O	O
?	?	O	O

Predicate : *di donlot* (EN: download)

token	vocab	gold	predicted
Jemma	Jemma	B-A	B-A
udah	udah	O	O
di	di	O	O
donlot	UNK	O	O
get	UNK	B-PS	O
rick	UNK	I-PS	O
nya	nya	I-PS	O

Table 4: Undetected Roles examples. Left translation: "This is a bot replying, right ?". Right translation: "Jemma, have you downloaded get rick?"

Predicate: *ada* (EN: exists)

token	vocab	gold	predicted
jem	jem	B-G	B-G
ada	ada	O	O
info	info	B-PS	B-PS
makanan	makanan	I-PS	O
gak	gak	O	O
?	?	O	O
.	.	O	O

Predicate: *tny* (EN : ask)

token	vocab	gold	predicted
Aku	Aku	B-A	B-A
mau	mau	O	O
tny	UNK	O	O
sahabar	UNK	B-PS	B-PS
virtual	virtual	I-PS	O
itu	itu	I-PS	O
mksd	mksd	O	O
a	a	O	O
gimana	gimana	O	O
?	?	O	O
.	.	O	O

Table 5: Boundary error examples. Top translation: "Jem, do you have any food related info?". Bottom translation: "I want to ask what is a virtual friend meaning?"

Predicate: *genit* (EN : flirt)

true	vocab	gold	pred
Jemma	Jemma	B-P	B-A
jangan	jangan	O	O
genit	UNK	O	O
sama	sama	O	O
NAME	UNK	B-BN	B-PS
;	UNK	O	O
(	(	O	O
.	.	O	O

Predicate: *lihat* (EN : see)

true	vocab	gold	predicted
Aku	Aku	O	B-A
kesal	UNK	O	O
lihat	lihat	O	O
kamu	kamu	B-G	B-BN
dek	UNK	B-PS	O
.	.	I-PS	O

Table 6: Role confusion examples. Top translation: "Jemma do not flirt with NAME (person name is censored due to privacy)". Bottom translation: "I am annoyed to see you boy[a]"

---

[a]In the original language, the word is gender neutral.

but not a mistyped word, the right sample's predicate "*di donlot*" is an informal writing of the word "download".

In the 50% training data scenario, we found that multi-task active learning model achieves less recall compared to the single-task active learning model. The multi-task active learning with 50% initial training data performance suffers from failing to tag 53% of BENEFACTOR label.

Boundary Error

Overall, we found that boundary errors contribute to 22% of the total span exact match errors. For example, we found that PATIENT boundary errors mostly occurred because predicted role spans do not match the continuation of subsequent role. As shown in Table 5, the model failed to recognize *makanan* (EN: food) as the continuation of *info* (EN: info) from the top example. In the bottom example, the model failed to predict the continuation of a mistyped role "*sahabar*".

Role Confusion

Role confusion is defined as the matching between gold span and predicted span, but they have different labels. This error typically occurs the least compared to the false negatives and boundary errors. In total, it is only 7% of the total errors. The most common incorrect prediction is between gold PATIENT and prediction AGENT. As shown in

Table 6 in the top sentence, the model incorrectly labeled a PATIENT (Jemma) as an AGENT. Additionally, the model also incorrectly tagged BENE-FACTOR as PATIENT. In the bottom sentence, the word *"Aku"* (EN: I) is not annotated as any roles but detected as an AGENT by the model.

6 Conclusion & Future Work

In this paper, we applied previous state-of-the-art deep semantic role labeling models on a low resource language in a conversational domain. We propose to combine multi-task and active learning methods into a single framework to achieve competitive SRL performance with less training data, and to leverage a semantically related task for SRL.

Our primary motivation is to apply the framework for low resource languages in terms of dataset size and domains. Our experiments demonstrate that active learning method performs comparably well to the single-task baseline using 30% fewer data by querying a total of 3483 from 4845 sentences. This result can be increased further marginally to outperform the baseline using 87% of the training data. Our error analysis reveals some different obstacles from English SRL to work on in the future.

While He et al.'s model of deep layers of highway LSTM allows learning the relation between a predicate and arguments explicitly, not all tasks in multi-task learning have equal complexity that needs deep layers. Søgaard and Goldberg (2016) proposed a method to allow a model to predict tasks with different complexities at different layer depths. For example, predicting entity recognition tag at lower layers or inserting predicate features at higher layers in an LSTM, because entity recognition does not need predicates as features and is considered as a lower-level task compared to SRL.

Combining multi-task learning with an unsupervised task such as language modeling (Rei, 2017) is also a possible improvement in multi-task active learning settings as a semi-supervised variant. Analyzing other active learning methods such as query by committee, variance reduction (Settles and Craven, 2008), and information density (Wang et al., 2017b) in multi-task settings are also a promising path in deep learning architectures.

References

Alan Akbik and Yunyao Li. 2016. K-srl: Instance-based learning for semantic role labeling. In *COLING*.

Rich Caruana. 1997. Multitask learning. *Machine Learning*, 28:41–75.

Jinho D. Choi, Claire Bonial, and Martha Palmer. 2010. Propbank frameset annotation guidelines using a dedicated editor, cornerstone. In *Proceedings of the Seventh International Conference on Language Resources and Evaluation (LREC'10)*, Valletta, Malta. European Language Resources Association (ELRA).

Ronan Collobert, Jason Weston, Léon Bottou, Michael Karlen, Koray Kavukcuoglu, and Pavel Kuksa. 2011. Natural language processing (almost) from scratch. *J. Mach. Learn. Res.*, 12:2493–2537.

Matthew R. Gormley, Margaret Mitchell, Benjamin Van Durme, and Mark Dredze. 2014. Low-resource semantic role labeling. In *ACL*.

Luheng He, Kenton Lee, Mike Lewis, and Luke Zettlemoyer. 2017. Deep semantic role labeling: What works and whats next. In *Proceedings of the Annual Meeting of the Association for Computational Linguistics*.

Luheng He, Mike Lewis, and Luke S. Zettlemoyer. 2015. Question-answer driven semantic role labeling: Using natural language to annotate natural language. In *EMNLP*.

Richard Johansson and Pierre Nugues. 2008. Dependency-based semantic role labeling of propbank. In *Proceedings of the Conference on Empirical Methods in Natural Language Processing*, EMNLP '08, pages 69–78, Stroudsburg, PA, USA. Association for Computational Linguistics.

Daniel Jurafsky and James H. Martin. 2006. Speech and language processing: an introduction to natural language processing, computational linguistics, and speech recognition.

John D. Lafferty, Andrew McCallum, and Fernando Pereira. 2001. Conditional random fields: Probabilistic models for segmenting and labeling sequence data. In *ICML*.

David D. Lewis and William A. Gale. 1994. A sequential algorithm for training text classifiers. In *SIGIR*.

Xuezhe Ma and Eduard H. Hovy. 2016. End-to-end sequence labeling via bi-directional lstm-cnns-crf. *CoRR*, abs/1603.01354.

Ana Marasovic and Anette Frank. 2017. SRL4ORL: improving opinion role labelling using multi-task learning with semantic role labeling. *CoRR*, abs/1711.00768.

Diego Marcheggiani and Thierry Artières. 2014. An experimental comparison of active learning strategies for partially labeled sequences. In *EMNLP*.

Tomas Mikolov, Kai Chen, Greg Corrado, and Jeffrey Dean. 2013. Efficient estimation of word representations in vector space. *arXiv preprint arXiv:1301.3781*.

Martha Palmer, Paul Kingsbury, and Daniel Gildea. 2005. The proposition bank: An annotated corpus of semantic roles. *Computational Linguistics*, 31:71–106.

Vasin Punyakanok, Dan Roth, Wen tau Yih, and Dav Zimak. 2004. Semantic role labeling via integer linear programming inference. In *COLING*.

Marek Rei. 2017. Semi-supervised multitask learning for sequence labeling. In *ACL*.

Roi Reichart, Katrin Tomanek, Udo Hahn, and Ari Rappoport. 2008. Multi-task active learning for linguistic annotations. In *Proceedings of ACL-08: HLT*, pages 861–869, Columbus, Ohio. Association for Computational Linguistics.

Nils Reimers and Iryna Gurevych. 2017. Reporting score distributions makes a difference: Performance study of lstm-networks for sequence tagging. In *EMNLP*.

Burr Settles. 2012. *Active Learning*. Morgan & Claypool, San Rafael, USA.

Burr Settles and Mark Craven. 2008. An analysis of active learning strategies for sequence labeling tasks. In *Proceedings of the Conference on Empirical Methods in Natural Language Processing*, EMNLP '08, pages 1070–1079, Stroudsburg, PA, USA. Association for Computational Linguistics.

Anders Søgaard and Yoav Goldberg. 2016. Deep multi-task learning with low level tasks supervised at lower layers. In *Proceedings of the 54th Annual Meeting of the Association for Computational Linguistics (Volume 2: Short Papers)*, pages 231–235. Association for Computational Linguistics.

Pontus Stenetorp, Sampo Pyysalo, Goran Topić, Tomoko Ohta, Sophia Ananiadou, and Jun'ichi Tsujii. 2012. brat: a web-based tool for NLP-assisted text annotation. In *Proceedings of the Demonstrations Session at EACL 2012*, Avignon, France. Association for Computational Linguistics.

Chenguang Wang, Alan Akbik, laura chiticariu, Yunyao Li, Fei Xia, and Anbang Xu. 2017a. Crowd-in-the-loop: A hybrid approach for annotating semantic roles. In *Proceedings of the 2017 Conference on Empirical Methods in Natural Language Processing*, pages 1914–1923. Association for Computational Linguistics.

Chenguang Wang, Laura Chiticariu, and Yunyao Li. 2017b. Active learning for black-box semantic role labeling with neural factors. In *IJCAI*.

Matthew D. Zeiler. 2012. Adadelta: An adaptive learning rate method. *CoRR*, abs/1212.5701.

Jie Zhou and Wei Xu. 2015. End-to-end learning of semantic role labeling using recurrent neural networks. In *Proceedings of the 53rd Annual Meeting of the Association for Computational Linguistics and the 7th International Joint Conference on Natural Language Processing (Volume 1: Long Papers)*, pages 1127–1137, Beijing, China. Association for Computational Linguistics.

Domain Adapted Word Embeddings for Improved Sentiment Classification

Prathusha K Sarma, Yingyu Liang and William A Sethares

University of Wisconsin-Madison
`{kameswarasar,sethares}@wisc.edu,`
`yliang@cs.wisc.edu`

Abstract

Generic word embeddings are trained on large-scale generic corpora; *Domain Specific* (DS) word embeddings are trained only on data from a domain of interest. This paper proposes a method to combine the breadth of generic embeddings with the specificity of domain specific embeddings. The resulting embeddings, called *Domain Adapted* (DA) word embeddings, are formed by first aligning corresponding word vectors using Canonical Correlation Analysis (CCA) or the related nonlinear Kernel CCA (KCCA) and then combining them via convex optimization. Results from evaluation on sentiment classification tasks show that the DA embeddings substantially outperform both generic, DS embeddings when used as input features to standard or state-of-the-art sentence encoding algorithms for classification.

1 Introduction

Generic word embeddings such as Glove and word2vec (Pennington et al., 2014; Mikolov et al., 2013) which are pre-trained on large bodies of raw text, have demonstrated remarkable success when used as features for supervised learning problems. There are, however, many applications with domain specific vocabularies and relatively small amounts of data. The performance of generic word embeddings in such applications is limited, since word embeddings pre-trained on generic corpora do not capture domain specific semantics/knowledge, while embeddings learned on small data sets are of low quality.

A concrete example of a small-sized domain specific corpus is the Substances User Disorders (SUDs) data set (Quanbeck et al., 2014; Litvin

et al., 2013), which contains messages on discussion forums for people with substance addictions. These forums are part of mobile health intervention treatments that encourages participants to engage in sobriety-related discussions. The goal of such treatments is to analyze content of participants' digital media content and provide human intervention via machine learning algorithms. This data is both domain specific and limited in size. Other examples include customer support tickets reporting issues with taxi-cab services, product reviews, reviews of restaurants and movies, discussions by special interest groups and political surveys. In general they are common in domains where words have different sentiment from what they would have elsewhere.

These data sets present significant challenges for word embedding learning algorithms. First, words in data on specific topics have a different distribution than words from generic corpora. Hence using generic word embeddings obtained from algorithms trained on a corpus such as Wikipedia, would introduce considerable errors in performance metrics on specific downstream tasks such as sentiment classification. For example, in SUDs, discussions are focused on topics related to recovery and addiction; the sentiment behind the word 'party' may be very different in a dating context than in a substance abuse context. Thus domain specific vocabularies and word semantics may be a problem for pre-trained sentiment classification models (Blitzer et al., 2007). Second, there is insufficient data to completely retrain a new set of word embeddings. The SUD data set consists of a few hundred people and only a fraction of these are active (Firth et al., 2017), (Naslund et al., 2015). This results in a small data set of text messages available for analysis. Furthermore, these messages are unstructured and the language used is informal. Fine-tuning the generic

Proceedings of the Workshop on Deep Learning Approaches for Low-Resource NLP, pages 51–59
Melbourne, Australia July 19, 2018. ©2018 Association for Computational Linguistics

word embedding also leads to noisy outputs due to the highly non-convex training objective and the small amount of the data. Since such data sets are common, a simple and effective method to adapt word embedding approaches is highly valuable. While existing work (e.g (Yin and Schütze, 2016)) combines word embeddings from different algorithms to improve upon intrinsic tasks such as similarities, analogies etc, there does not exist a concrete method to combine multiple embeddings for extrinsic tasks. This paper proposes a method for obtaining high quality domain adapted word embeddings that capture domain specific semantics and are suitable for tasks on the specific domain. Our contributions are as follows.

1. We propose an algorithm to obtain Domain Adapted (DA) embeddings. DA embeddings are obtained by performing three steps. (i) First, generic embeddings are obtained from algorithms such as Glove or word2vec that are trained large corpora (such as wikipedia, common crawl). (ii) Next we learn domain specific (DS) embeddings by applying algorithms such as Latent Semantic Analysis (LSA) on the domain specific corpus. (iii) We then perform Canonical Correlation Analysis (CCA) or kernelized CCA (KCCA) to obtain projected DS and projected generic embeddings. The projected DS and generic embeddings are linearly combined via an optimization formulation to obtain a single DA embedding for each word.

2. We propose two optimization based approaches to combining generic and DS embeddings. In the first method, we minimize the sum of squared distance of the DA embeddings from the projected embeddings. The second approach combines projected embeddings in such a way that the document clusters are tightly packed. This helps in our downstream sentiment analysis task by separating out the clusters.

3. We demonstrate the efficacy of our embeddings by measuring the accuracy of our classifiers built using various embeddings on a sentiment analysis task. In the first set of experiments (Table (1)) we train logistic regression classifiers using a bag-of-words (BOW) framework, for the problem of sentiment analysis. Our experimental results show

that the classifier built using DA word embeddings outperform the classifiers built using Glove, word2vec or LSA. Our classifier also outperforms the classifier built using the embeddings output by the concSVD algorithm (Yin and Schütze, 2016) which, obtains a word embedding by performing SVD on a matrix of word embeddings.

4. In the second set of experiments we demonstrate the efficiency of DA embeddings when used to initialize InferSent; a bi-LSTM, encoder/decoder architecture that learns sentence embeddings from input word embeddings. The resulting document embeddings are classified using logistic regression classifier. Performance metrics (see Table (2)) show that DA embeddings outperform generic embeddings such as Glove common crawl, when used to initialize InferSent. Furthermore, we also outperform RNTN, which is a recursive neural network based sentiment analysis algorithm (Socher et al., 2013).

The remainder of this paper is organized as follows. Section 2 presents related work. Section 3 briefly introduces the CCA/KCCA and details the procedure used to obtain the DA embeddings. Section 4 describes the experimental set up and discusses the results from sentiment classification tasks on benchmark data sets using standard classification as well as using a sentence encoding algorithm. Section 5 concludes this work.

2   Related Work

This work is related to three areas of research which are outlined below.

CCA based word embeddings and applications in multilingual correlation: In (Dhillon et al., 2012), the authors proposed an algorithm called Two Step CCA to learn word embeddings from a one hot encoding representation of words in a given vocabulary. CCA has been used to learn multilingual word embeddings (Faruqui and Dyer, 2014) from words aligned in text across different languages. Building on this work, (Lu et al., 2015) developed deep CCA to learn multilingual word embeddings using neural networks. In both these algorithms, word embeddings are learned for words and their translations across multiple languages such as English-German or English-

French, separately via a LSA based approach. Embeddings in the two different languages are then projected onto the best k correlated dimensions via CCA.

Recently, (Gouws et al., 2015) proposed a neural network based model that learns across multiple languages without the need for word alignment. This algorithm jointly optimizes learning of monolingual embeddings via an objective similar to (Mikolov et al., 2013), along with a cross lingual alignment task. Recently, CCA has been applied to perform cross-lingual entity linking tasks (Tsai and Roth, 2016).

Most applications of CCA in NLP, as stated above, have focused on multilingual settings. In contrast, in this paper we use CCA/KCCA to improve performance of monolingual word embeddings across data sets in different application domains/contexts for the purpose of a given downstream task such as sentiment classification.

Domain Adaptation with CCA: The idea of using word embeddings across different domains has been explored by (Luo et al., 2014) where word embeddings are learned independently from two large corpora and then combined via a neural network. This is different from our approach where the CCA-based approach is used to exploit co-occurrences and context information in the domain specific data set along with linear properties of the generic word embedding. More recently, (Yin and Schütze, 2016) propose an ensemble approach of combining word embeddings learned via different embedding algorithms across different data sets. One of their proposed approaches is to concatenate word vectors from multiple embeddings and to then performing SVD on the resulting matrix. The resulting embeddings are then evaluated on several intrinsic tasks such as word similarities and analogies. In contrast, our work focuses on adapting the word vectors to incorporate domain specific knowledge which is important for the extrinsic objective of sentiment classification. In Section (4) we compare our algorithms against the algorithms of (Yin and Schütze, 2016) and show that we outperform (Yin and Schütze, 2016) for the task of sentiment analysis. Some other work (Blitzer et al., 2011), (Anoop et al., 2015) and (Mehrkanoon and Suykens, 2017) explores CCA based dimensionality reduction techniques for domain adaptation in problems with multi-modal data in general, but not necessarily

natural language data.

Transfer Learning using Sentence Embeddings: The idea of training on a large corpus and testing on a different yet related data set has been successfully explored via transfer learning in computer vision applications (Taigman et al., 2014; Sharif Razavian et al., 2014; Antol et al., 2015). A similar idea has been explored to solve problems in NLP applications via sentence level embeddings with and without composition of word embeddings. An unsupervised algorithm such as skip-thought (Kiros et al., 2015) that adapts the word level skip-gram model by (Mikolov et al., 2013) to sentence level embeddings has demonstrated success in transfer learning tasks. Similarly, (Hill et al., 2016) compare task-specific sentence embeddings to supervised methods for applications on machine translation data.

However, these supervised models fail to perform as well as an unsupervised Skip-Net. The current state-of-the art in sentence embedding algorithms is InferSent (Conneau et al., 2017), which learns a sentence embedding via an encoder trained on the Stanford Natural Language Inference data set. It has demonstrated success in many transfer tasks. While domain adaptation is not the focus of these algorithms, the underlying idea of training a model on one data set/task and testing on a different data set/task is relevant to the theme of this paper. In fact, our experiments demonstrate that our domain adapted embeddings combined with the InferSent architecture can significantly improve over generic embeddings combined with InferSent in the sentiment classification task.

3 Domain Adapted Word Embeddings

Training word embedding algorithms on small data sets leads to noisy outputs, due to lack of data, while embeddings from generic corpora fail to capture specific local meanings within the domain. For example, the word "alcohol" has a somewhat neutral to a mildly positive tone in the common crawl corpus, whereas this same word has a strong negative sentiment in a substance use disorder (SUD) dataset. In order to learn useful word embeddings that incorporate the sentimentality of a small target corpus, we propose learning domain specific embeddings obtained by applying word embedding algorithms on the given target corpus and generic embeddings, obtained using applying word embedding algorithms on large generic corpora, using CCA or kernel CCA (KCCA).

Let $\mathbf{W}_{DS} \in \mathbb{R}^{|V_{DS}| \times d_1}$ be the matrix whose columns are the domain specific word embeddings (obtained by, e.g., the LSA algorithm on the domain specific data set), where V_{DS} is its vocabulary and d_1 is the dimension of the embeddings. Similarly, let $\mathbf{W}_G \in \mathbb{R}^{|V_G| \times d_2}$ be the matrix of generic word embeddings (obtained by, e.g., GloVe algorithm on the Common Crawl data), where V_G is the vocabulary and d_2 is the dimension of the embeddings. Let $V_\cap = V_{DS} \cap V_G$. Let $\mathbf{w}_{i,DS}$ be the domain specific embedding of the word $i \in V_\cap$, and $\mathbf{w}_{i,G}$ be its generic embedding. For one dimensional CCA, let ϕ_{DS} and ϕ_G be the projection directions of $\mathbf{w}_{i,DS}$ and $\mathbf{w}_{i,G}$ respectively. Then the projected values are,

$$\bar{w}_{i,DS} = \mathbf{w}_{i,DS}\,\phi_{DS}$$
$$\bar{w}_{i,G} = \mathbf{w}_{i,G}\,\phi_G. \tag{1}$$

CCA maximizes the correlation ρ between $\bar{w}_{i,DS}$ and $\bar{w}_{i,G}$ to obtain ϕ_{DS} and ϕ_G such that

$$\rho(\phi_{DS}, \phi_G) = \max_{\phi_{DS}, \phi_G} \frac{\mathbb{E}[\bar{w}_{i,DS}\bar{w}_{i,G}]}{\sqrt{\mathbb{E}[\bar{w}_{i,DS}^2]\mathbb{E}[\bar{w}_{i,G}^2]}} \tag{2}$$

where the expectation is over all words $i \in V_\cap$.

The d-dimensional CCA with $d > 1$ can be defined recursively. Suppose the first $d - 1$ pairs of canonical variables are defined. Then the dth pair is defined by seeking vectors maximizing the same correlation function subject to the constraint that they be uncorrelated with the first $d - 1$ pairs. Equivalently, matrices of projection vectors $\mathbf{\Phi}_{DS} \in \mathbb{R}^{d_1 \times d}$ and $\mathbf{\Phi}_G \in \mathbb{R}^{d_2 \times d}$ are obtained for all vectors in $\mathbf{W}_{DS}$ and $\mathbf{W}_G$ where $d \leq \min\{d_1, d_2\}$. Embeddings obtained by $\bar{\mathbf{w}}_{i,DS} = \mathbf{w}_{i,DS}\,\mathbf{\Phi}_{DS}$ and $\bar{\mathbf{w}}_{i,G} = \mathbf{w}_{i,G}\,\mathbf{\Phi}_G$ are projections along the directions of maximum correlation. The final domain adapted embedding for word i is given by $\hat{\mathbf{w}}_{i,DA} = \alpha\bar{\mathbf{w}}_{i,DS} + \beta\bar{\mathbf{w}}_{i,G}$. We next propose optimization based algorithms to determine α, β.

3.1 α, β that minimizes the sum of squared distances

One way to determine α and β is to find DA embeddings such that in the CCA transformed space, the new DA embeddings are as close as possible to both generic and DS embeddings. This is ex-pressed by the following optimization problem,

$$\min_{\alpha, \beta} \|\bar{\mathbf{w}}_{i,DS} - (\alpha\bar{\mathbf{w}}_{i,DS} + \beta\bar{\mathbf{w}}_{i,G})\|_2^2 +$$
$$\|\bar{\mathbf{w}}_{i,G} - (\alpha\bar{\mathbf{w}}_{i,DS} + \beta\bar{\mathbf{w}}_{i,G})\|_2^2. \tag{3}$$

Solving (3) gives $\alpha = \beta = \frac{1}{2}$, i.e., the new vector is equal to the average of the two projections:

$$\hat{\mathbf{w}}_{i,DA} = \frac{1}{2}\bar{\mathbf{w}}_{i,DS} + \frac{1}{2}\bar{\mathbf{w}}_{i,G}. \tag{4}$$

3.2 α, β to minimize the sum of cluster variance

A major goal of learning domain adapted embeddings is to use them in a downstream task such as sentiment analysis. To facilitate better sentiment analysis it helps if the cluster of positive and negative documents are tightly clustered. That is, we would like to minimize the sum of variance of each individual cluster of documents. This can be cast as a convex optimization problem that has a closed form solution as shown in the following theorem.

Theorem 1. *Let $\beta = 1 - \alpha$. Then, the optimal value of α that minimizes the sum of the variance of document clusters is given by the following set of equations,*
$$\tilde{\alpha} = \frac{\frac{1}{k}\sum_{i=1}^{k}(d_{gp_i} - \hat{\mu}_p)^\top(\bar{\mu}_p - \bar{d}_{p_i}) + \frac{1}{N-k}\sum_{i=1}^{N-k}(d_{gn_i} - \hat{\mu}_n)^\top(\bar{\mu}_n - \bar{d}_{n_i})}{\frac{1}{k}\sum_{i=1}^{k}(\bar{\mu}_p - \bar{d}_{p_i})^\top(\bar{\mu}_p - \bar{d}_{p_i}) + \frac{1}{N-k}\sum_{i=1}^{N-k}(\bar{\mu}_n - \bar{d}_{n_i})^\top(\bar{\mu}_n - \bar{d}_{n_i})}$$
$$\alpha = \max(0, \min(\tilde{\alpha}, 1)).$$

Proof. Assume that a DA embedding is expressed as, $\hat{\mathbf{w}}_{i,DA} = \alpha\bar{\mathbf{w}}_{i,DS} + (1 - \alpha)\bar{\mathbf{w}}_{i,G}$. Further, let each ith document be expressed as the sum of constituent word embeddings,

$$d_i = \sum_{j=1}^{n} \hat{\mathbf{w}}_{j,DA}$$
$$= \sum_{j=1}^{n} (\bar{\mathbf{w}}_{j,G} + \alpha(\bar{\mathbf{w}}_{j,DS} - \bar{\mathbf{w}}_{j,G}))$$
$$= d_{g_i} + \alpha\bar{d}_i.$$

Suppose, there are N documents of which k are positive and $N - k$ are negative. Also, let μ_p, μ_n denote the cluster center of all positive and negative documents respectively. We can determine α that minimizes the sum of cluster variances by solving

$$\min_{\alpha \in [0,1]} \frac{1}{k}\sum_{i=1}^{k} \|d_{p_i} - \mu_p\|_2^2 + \frac{1}{N-k}\sum_{i=1}^{N-k} \|d_{n_i} - \mu_n\|_2^2 \tag{5}$$

Here μ_p and μ_n are centers of positive and negative document cluster centers. Taking means of clusters, we get $\mu_p = \frac{1}{k}\sum_{i=1}^{k}(d_{g_{p_i}} + \alpha \bar{d}_{p_i}) = \hat{\mu}_p + \alpha\bar{\mu}_p$. Similarly $\mu_n = \hat{\mu}_n + \alpha\bar{\mu}_n$.

$$\min_{\alpha\in[0,1]} \frac{1}{k}\sum_{i=1}^{k} \|(d_{g_{p_i}} - \hat{\mu}_p) - \alpha(\bar{\mu}_p - \bar{d}_{p_i})\|_2^2 +$$
$$\frac{1}{N-k}\sum_{i=1}^{N-k} \|(d_{g_{n_i}} - \hat{\mu}_n) - \alpha(\bar{\mu}_n - \bar{d}_{n_i})\|_2^2. \quad (6)$$

The above problem is a very simple convex minimization problem. Differentiating w.r.t. α and setting it to 0, and projecting the resulting solution onto the interval $[0,1]$ we get the desired result. $\quad\square$

3.3 Kernel CCA

Because of its linear structure, the CCA in (2) may not always capture the best relationships between the two matrices. To account for nonlinearities, a kernel function, which implicitly maps the data into a high dimensional feature space, can be applied. For example, given a vector $\mathbf{w} \in \mathbb{R}^d$, a kernel function K is written in the form of a feature map φ defined by $\varphi : \mathbf{w} = (\mathbf{w}_1, \ldots, \mathbf{w}_d) \mapsto \varphi(\mathbf{w}) = (\varphi_1(\mathbf{w}), \ldots, \varphi_m(\mathbf{w}))(d < m)$ such that given $\mathbf{w}_a$ and $\mathbf{w}_b$

$$K(\mathbf{w}_a, \mathbf{w}_b) = \langle \varphi(\mathbf{w}_a), \varphi(\mathbf{w}_b) \rangle.$$

In kernel CCA, data is first projected onto a high dimensional feature space before performing CCA. In this work the kernel function used is a Gaussian kernel, i.e.,

$$K(\mathbf{w}_a, \mathbf{w}_b) = \exp\left(-\frac{\|\mathbf{w}_a - \mathbf{w}_b\|^2}{2\sigma^2}\right).$$

The implementation of kernel CCA follows the standard algorithm described in several texts such as (Hardoon et al., 2004); see reference for details.

4 Experimental Evaluation

In this section we evaluate DA embeddings in binary sentiment classification tasks on four standard data sets. Document embeddings are obtained via i) a standard bag-of-words framework, in which documents are expressed as the weighted combination of their constituent word embeddings and ii) by initializing a state-of-the-art-sentence encoding algorithm, InferSent (Conneau et al.,

Data Set		Embedding	Avg Precision	Avg F-score	Avg AUC
Yelp	$\mathbf{W}_{DA}$	KCCA(Glv, LSA)	85.36± 2.8	81.89±2.8	82.57±1.3
		CCA(Glv, LSA)	83.69± 4.7	79.48±2.4	80.33±2.9
		KCCA(w2v, LSA)	87.45± 1.2	83.36±1.2	84.10±0.9
		CCA(w2v, LSA)	84.52± 2.3	80.02±2.6	81.04±2.1
		KCCA(GlvCC, LSA)	**88.11± 3.0**	**85.35±2.7**	**85.80±2.4**
		CCA(GlvCC, LSA)	83.69± 3.5	78.99±4.2	80.03±3.7
		KCCA(w2v, DSw2v)	78.09± 1.7	76.04±1.7	76.66±1.5
		CCA(w2v, DSw2v)	86.22± 3.5	84.35±2.4	84.65±2.2
		concSVD(Glv, LSA)	80.14± 2.6	78.50±3.0	78.92±2.7
		concSVD(w2v, LSA)	85.11± 2.3	83.51±2.2	83.80±2.0
		concSVD(GlvCC, LSA)	84.20± 3.7	80.39±3.7	80.83±3.9
	$\mathbf{W}_{G}$	GloVe	77.13± 4.2	72.32±7.9	74.17±5.0
		GloVe-CC	82.10± 3.5	76.74±3.4	78.17±2.7
		word2vec	82.80± 3.5	78.28±3.5	79.35±3.1
	$\mathbf{W}_{DS}$	LSA	75.36± 5.4	71.17±4.3	72.57±4.3
		word2vec	73.08± 2.2	70.97±2.4	71.76±2.1
Amazon	$\mathbf{W}_{DA}$	KCCA(Glv, LSA)	86.30±1.9	83.00±2.9	83.39±3.2
		CCA(Glv, LSA)	84.68±2.4	82.27±2.2	82.78±1.7
		KCCA(w2v, LSA)	87.09±1.8	82.63±2.6	83.50±2.0
		CCA(w2v, LSA)	84.80±1.5	81.42±1.9	82.12±1.3
		KCCA(GlvCC, LSA)	**89.73±2.4**	85.47±2.4	85.56±2.6
		CCA(GlvCC, LSA)	85.67±2.3	83.83±2.3	84.21±2.1
		KCCA(w2v, DSw2v)	85.68±3.2	81.23±3.2	82.20±2.9
		CCA(w2v, DSw2v)	83.50±3.4	81.31±4.0	81.86±3.7
		concSVD(Glv, LSA)	82.36±2.0	81.30±3.5	81.51±2.5
		concSVD(w2v, LSA)	87.28±2.9	**86.17±2.5**	**86.42±2.0**
		concSVD(GlvCC, LSA)	84.93±1.6	77.81±2.3	79.52±1.7
	$\mathbf{W}_{G}$	GloVe	81.58±2.5	77.62±2.7	78.72±2.7
		GloVe-CC	79.91±2.7	81.63±2.8	81.46±2.6
		word2vec	84.55±1.9	80.52±2.5	81.45±2.0
	$\mathbf{W}_{DS}$	LSA	82.65±4.4	73.92±3.8	76.40±3.2
		word2vec	74.20±5.8	72.49±5.0	73.11±4.8
IMDB	DA	KCCA(Glv, LSA)	73.84±1.3	73.07±3.6	73.17±2.4
		CCA(Glv, LSA)	73.35±2.0	73.00±3.2	73.06±2.0
		KCCA(w2v, LSA)	**82.36±4.4**	**78.95±2.7**	**79.66±2.6**
		CCA(w2v, LSA)	80.66±4.5	75.95±4.5	77.23±3.8
		KCCA(GlvCC, LSA)	54.50±2.5	54.42±2.9	53.91±2.0
		CCA(GlvCC, LSA)	54.08±2.0	53.03±3.5	54.90±2.1
		KCCA(w2v, DSw2v)	60.65±3.5	58.95±3.2	58.95±3.7
		CCA(w2v, DSw2v)	58.47±2.7	57.62±3.0	58.03±3.9
		concSVD(Glv, LSA)	73.25±3.7	74.55±3.2	73.02±4.7
		concSVD(w2v, LSA)	53.87±2.2	51.77±5.8	53.54±1.9
		concSVD(GlvCC, LSA)	78.28±3.2	77.67±3.7	74.55±2.9
	$\mathbf{W}_{G}$	GloVe	64.44±2.6	65.18±3.5	64.62±2.6
		GloVe-CC	50.53±1.8	62.39±3.5	49.96±2.3
		word2vec	78.92±3.7	74.88±3.1	75.60±2.4
	$\mathbf{W}_{DS}$	LSA	67.92±1.7	69.79±5.3	69.71±3.8
		word2vec	56.87±3.6	56.04±3.1	59.53±8.9
A-CHESS	DA	**KCCA(Glv, LSA)**	32.07±1.3	39.32±2.5	**65.96±1.3**
		CCA(Glv, LSA)	32.70±1.5	35.48±4.2	62.15±2.9
		KCCA(w2v, LSA)	33.45±1.3	**39.81±1.0**	65.92±0.6
		CCA(w2v, LSA)	33.06±3.2	34.02±1.1	60.91±0.9
		KCCA(GlvCC, LSA)	36.38±1.2	34.71±4.8	61.36±2.6
		CCA(GlvCC, LSA)	32.11±2.9	36.85±4.4	62.99±3.1
		KCCA(w2v, DSw2v)	25.59±1.2	28.27±3.1	57.25±1.7
		CCA(w2v, DSw2v)	24.88±1.4	29.17±3.1	57.76±2.0
		concSVD(Glv, LSA)	27.27±2.9	34.45±3.0	61.59±2.3
		concSVD(w2v, LSA)	29.84±2.3	36.32±3.3	62.94±1.1
		concSVD(GlvCC, LSA)	28.09±1.9	35.06±1.4	62.13±2.6
	$\mathbf{W}_{G}$	GloVe	30.82±2.0	33.67±3.4	60.80±2.3
		GloVe-CC	**38.13±0.8**	27.45±3.1	57.49±1.2
		word2vec	32.67±2.9	31.72±1.6	59.64±0.5
	$\mathbf{W}_{DS}$	LSA	27.42±1.6	34.38±2.3	61.56±1.9
		word2vec	24.48±0.8	27.97±3.7	57.08±2.5

Table 1: This table shows results from the classification task using sentence embeddings obtained from weighted averaging of word embeddings. Metrics reported are average Precision, F-score and AUC and the corresponding standard deviations. Best performing embeddings and corresponding metrics are highlighted in boldface.

2017) with DA word embeddings to obtain sentence embeddings. Encoded sentences are then classified using a logistic regressor. Performance metrics reported are average precision, F-score and AUC. All hyperparameters are tuned via 10 fold cross validation.

4.1 Data Sets

Experiments are conducted using four data sets which differ in vocabulary and content. All four arise in specific domains and hence illustrate the objective of this work. The four data sets are:

- The **Yelp data set** consists of 1000 restaurant reviews obtained from Yelp. Each review is associated with a 'positive' or 'negative' label. There are a total of 2049 distinct word tokens in this data set.

- The **Amazon data set** consists of 1000 product reviews with 'positive' or 'negative' labels obtained from Amazon. It has 1865 distinct tokens.

- The **IMDB data set** consists of 1000 movie reviews with binary 'positive' and 'negative' labels obtained from IMDB. It has 3075 distinct tokens.

- The **A-CHESS data set** is a proprietary data set[1] obtained from a study involving users with alcohol addiction. Text data is obtained from a discussion forum in the A-CHESS mobile app (Quanbeck et al., 2014). There are a total of 2500 text messages, with 8% of the messages indicative of relapse risk. Since this data set is part of a clinical trial, an exact text message cannot be provided as an example. However, the following messages illustrate typical messages in this data set, *"I've been clean for about 7 months but even now I still feel like maybe I won't make it."* Such a message is marked as 'threat' by a human moderator. On the other hand there are other benign messages that are marked 'not threat' such as *"30 days sober and counting, I feel like I am getting my life back."* The aim is to eventually automate this process since human moderation involves considerable effort and time. This is an unbalanced data set (8%

of the messages are marked 'threat') with a total of 3400 distinct work tokens.

The first three data sets are obtained from (Kotzias et al., 2015).

4.2 Word embeddings, baselines and parameter settings

The following generic and DS word embeddings are used,

- **Generic word embeddings:** Generic word embeddings used are GloVe[2] from both Wikipedia and common crawl and the word2vec (Skip-gram) embeddings[3]. These generic embeddings will be denoted as Glv, GlvCC and w2v.

- **DS word embeddings:** DS embeddings are obtained via Latent Semantic Analysis (LSA) and via retraining word2vec on the test data sets using the implementation in gensim[4]. DS embeddings via LSA are denoted by LSA and DS embeddings via word2vec are denoted by DSw2v. We also retrained GloVe on our test datasets to obtain domain specific word embeddings. Since, the performance of retrained Glove embeddings was similar to word2vec we shall not present the results of Glove based DS embeddings in this paper.

- **concatenation-SVD (concSVD) baseline:** Generic and DS embeddings are concatenated to form a single embeddings matrix. SVD is performed on this matrix and the resulting singular vectors are projected onto the d largest singular values to form word embeddings. The resultant word embeddings called meta-embeddings proposed by (Yin and Schütze, 2016) have demonstrated considerable success in intrinsic tasks such as similarities, analogies etc.

Dimensions of generic, DS and DA word embeddings are provided in the supplement.

Kernel parameter estimation A rule-of-thumb for estimating the kernel parameter σ is to set σ equal to the median of pairwise distance between data points (Flaxman et al., 2016). We use this rule

---

[1]Center for Health Enhancement System Services at UW-Madison

[2]https://nlp.stanford.edu/projects/glove/

[3]https://code.google.com/archive/p/word2vec/

[4]https://radimrehurek.com/gensim/

to set the value of σ for all of our experiments that use kernel CCA. CCA is performed using the readily available installation in python. KCCA used in this work is implemented in python and follows closely the implementation developed by (Bilenko and Gallant, 2016).

Data Set	Embedding	Avg Precision	Avg F-score	Avg AUC
Yelp	GlvCC	86.47±1.9	83.51±2.6	83.83±2.2
	KCCA(GlvCC, LSA)	**91.06±0.8**	**88.66±2.4**	**88.76±2.4**
	CCA(GlvCC, LSA)	86.26±1.4	82.61±1.1	83.99±0.8
	concSVD(GlvCC,LSA)	85.53±2.1	84.90±1.7	84.96±1.5
	RNTN	83.11±1.1	-	-
Amazon	GlvCC	87.93±2.7	82.41±3.3	83.24±2.8
	KCCA(GlvCC, LSA)	**90.56±2.1**	**86.52±2.0**	**86.74±1.9**
	CCA(GlvCC, LSA)	87.12±2.6	83.18±2.2	83.78±2.1
	concSVD(GlvCC, LSA)	85.73±1.9	85.19±2.4	85.17±2.6
	RNTN	82.84±0.6	-	-
IMDB	GlvCC	54.02±3.2	53.03±5.2	53.01±2.0
	KCCA(GlvCC, LSA)	59.76±7.3	**53.26±6.1**	56.46±3.4
	CCA(GlvCC, LSA)	53.62±1.6	50.62±5.1	**58.75±3.7**
	concSVD(GlvCC, LSA)	52.75±2.3	53.05±6.0	53.54±2.5
	RNTN	**80.88±0.7**	-	-
A-CHESS	GlvCC	52.21±5.1	**55.26±5.6**	**74.28±3.6**
	KCCA(GlvCC, LSA)	**55.37±5.5**	50.67±5.0	69.89±3.1
	CCA(GlvCC, LSA)	54.34±3.6	48.76±2.9	68.78±2.4
	concSVD(GlvCC, LSA)	40.41±4.2	44.75±5.2	68.13±3.8
	RNTN	-	-	-

Table 2: This table shows results obtained by initializing InferSent encoder with different embeddings in the sentiment classification task. Metrics reported are average Precision, F-score and AUC along with the corresponding standard deviations. Best performing embeddings and corresponding metrics are highlighted in boldface We use $\alpha = 0.5$ for all of our experiments here.

4.3 Results from standard classification tasks

Table 1 presents results from the standard classification task. In this approach, we use a bag-of-words approach to combine word embeddings weighted by their term frequency counts. The resulting encoding $v = \gamma^\top \mathbf{W}$. Here $\gamma \in \mathbb{R}^{|V|}$ represents the weights for all the words in the sentence/document, and $\mathbf{W}$ is the matrix whose columns are word embeddings. A logistic regression classifier is then trained on the training data and used to predict the sentiment labels on the test data sets. From this table, it can be inferred that DA embeddings obtained by applying KCCA on GlvCC generic and LSA DS embeddings provide the best performing results on all data sets. Note that in these experiments $\alpha = \frac{1}{2}$ (3.1). On the Amazon data set, concSVD achieves slightly better average F-score (86.17) and average AUC (86.42) over average F-score (85.47) and average AUC (85.56) obtained by KCCA (GlvCC, LSA). However, KCCA (GlvCC, LSA) achieves an average precision of 89.73 while concSVD achieves an average precision of 87.28. On the A-CHESS

data set, owing to the imbalance in the classes, the best performing embedding is one that achieves maximum precision. From the table we can determine that KCCA (GlvCC, LSA) achieves the highest average precision of 36.38.

4.4 Results from InferSent encoding for classification

In this section DA embeddings are used to initialize a state-of-the-art sentence encoding algorithm, InferSent. The resultant sentence embeddings are then classified using a logistic regression classifier. Table 2 presents results from classifying sentences obtained from InferSent. First, the pre-trained encoder[5] initialized with GloVe common crawl embeddings is used to obtain vector representations of the input data. Next, InferSent is fine-tuned with a combination of GloVe common crawl embeddings and DA embeddings. DA embeddings are only obtained for a small subset of a vocabulary, so the combination is obtained by using the common crawl embeddings for the rest of the vocabulary. The same procedure is repeated with concSVD embeddings. Additionally, embeddings are compared against a classic sentiment classification algorithm, the Recursive Neural Tensor Network (RNTN) (Socher et al., 2013). This is a dependency parser based sentiment analysis algorithm. Since the focus of this work is not on sentiment analysis algorithms per se, but on domain adaptation of word embeddings for extrinsic tasks, this is used as a baseline for comparison. From table 2 it can be inferred that KCCA(GlvCC, LSA) embeddings perform better than all other baselines for Yelp, Amazon and A-CHESS data sets. On the IMDB data set, RNTN performs best. This could be a case of (GlvCC, LSA) being bad initial guess embeddings for the IMDB data set. Performance of GlvCC embeddings from table 1 further support this conjecture. Also, InferSent produces superior sentence embeddings than simple averaging hence results from table 2 are better than results in table 1.

4.5 Results from using α that minimizes the sum of cluster variances

As described in Theorem (1), α can be selected to minimizes variance of document clusters when learning DA embeddings. Since from tables 1

[5] https://github.com/facebookresearch/InferSent

and 2 we see that the best performing DA embedding is obtained by KCCA, results for this embedding alone are presented in table 3. Furthermore, empirically we did not observe much difference in CCA DA embeddings obtained using $\alpha = 0.5$ and α that minimizes the sum of cluster variances. From tables 2 and 3 observe that on the Yelp, Amazon and IMDB data sets, there is not much of difference in performance metrics for $\alpha = 0.5$ and the α obtained from Theorem (1). However, on the A-CHESS data set, α as obtained from Theorem (1) does better than $\alpha = 0.5$. This result is not surprising given that the word sentiments on the A-CHESS data set is highly atypical. This supports our hypothesis that using only generic embeddings such as the GloVe common crawl is not sufficient when analyzing datasets such as the A-CHESS dataset.

Data Set	Embedding	α	Avg Precision	Avg F-score	Avg AUC
Yelp	KCCA(Glv, LSA)	0.25	84.75±2.2	80.02±2.5	81.13±2.0
	KCCA(w2v, LSA)	0.45	87.74±2.2	83.57±2.6	84.27±2.4
	KCCA(GlvCC, LSA)	0.6	88.84±2.3	85.36±2.3	85.93±2.0
Amazon	KCCA(Glv, LSA)	0.35	85.63±1.3	84.64±1.9	84.84±1.6
	KCCA(w2v, LSA)	0.54	87.15±2.0	84.27±1.9	84.79±1.6
	KCCA(GlvCC, LSA)	0.4	90.42±2.2	87.48±2.3	87.92±2.0
IMDB	KCCA(Glv, LSA)	0.35	72.10±1.8	72.63±2.3	73.01±2.1
	KCCA(w2v, LSA)	0.4	83.01±1.6	79.10±1.2	79.96±2.0
	KCCA(GlvCC, LSA)	0.45	58.56±1.8	53.29±1.7	60.56±1.9
A-CHESS	KCCA(Glv, LSA)	0.4	37.32±1.6	41.64±2.8	66.13±2.1
	KCCA(w2v, LSA)	0.55	35.06±0.9	43.44±1.4	68.60±1.3
	KCCA(GlvCC, LSA)	0.75	38.65±3.1	43.03±2.2	67.26±2.2

Table 3: This table shows results using KCCA DA embeddings within a BoW framework. Since from tables 1 and 2 we see that the best performing DA embedding is obtained by KCCA, results for this embedding alone are presented in this table. α used minimizes the sum of cluster variances as shown in Theorem (1). Note that on the A-CHESS dataset the value of α is large. This observation supports our hypothesis that on domain specific data sets such as A-CHESS, using only generic embeddings such as the GloVe common crawl, as features for classification or to initialize algorithms such as InferSent is not sufficient.

5 Discussion and Conclusion

In this paper DA embeddings are obtained by optimizing a combination of generic and DS embeddings that are projected along directions of maximum correlation. The resulting DA embeddings are evaluated on sentiment classification tasks from four different data sets. Results show that while actual performance metrics vary from database to database, the optimized DA embeddings outperform both the generic and the DS word embeddings in a standard classification framework; as well as outperform concatenation based combination embeddings. This is a positive results since CCA/KCCA provides a principled formulation for combining multiple embeddings. In contrast, concatenating embeddings followed by SVD is an ad-hoc procedure and does not exploit correlations among multiple embeddings. The need for such DA embeddings is motivated by the limitations of performance of generic embeddings on data sets such as A-CHESS. Initializing InferSent with DA embeddings further improves the output from InferSent. This is encouraging because several NLP tasks such as Sentiment Analysis, POS tagging, etc., use algorithms that must be initialized with word embeddings. Initializing such algorithms with embeddings customized to a particular domain or data set will improve performance of these algorithms. Future work will explore effectiveness of using our approach in other downstream applications such as question/answering, machine translation.

References

KR Anoop, Ramanathan Subramanian, Vassilios Vonikakis, KR Ramakrishnan, and Stefan Winkler. 2015. On the utility of canonical correlation analysis for domain adaptation in multi-view headpose estimation. In *Image Processing (ICIP), 2015 IEEE International Conference on*. IEEE, pages 4708–4712.

Stanislaw Antol, Aishwarya Agrawal, Jiasen Lu, Margaret Mitchell, Dhruv Batra, C Lawrence Zitnick, and Devi Parikh. 2015. Vqa: Visual question answering. In *Proceedings of the IEEE International Conference on Computer Vision*. pages 2425–2433.

Natalia Y Bilenko and Jack L Gallant. 2016. Pyrcca: regularized kernel canonical correlation analysis in python and its applications to neuroimaging. *Frontiers in neuroinformatics* 10.

John Blitzer, Mark Dredze, Fernando Pereira, et al. 2007. Biographies, bollywood, boom-boxes and blenders: Domain adaptation for sentiment classification. In *ACL*. volume 7, pages 440–447.

John Blitzer, Sham Kakade, and Dean Foster. 2011. Domain adaptation with coupled subspaces. In *Proceedings of the Fourteenth International Conference on Artificial Intelligence and Statistics*. pages 173–181.

Alexis Conneau, Douwe Kiela, Holger Schwenk, Loic Barrault, and Antoine Bordes. 2017. Supervised learning of universal sentence representations from natural language inference data. *arXiv preprint arXiv:1705.02364* .

Paramveer Dhillon, Jordan Rodu, Dean Foster, and Lyle Ungar. 2012. Two step cca: A new spectral method for estimating vector models of words. *arXiv preprint arXiv:1206.6403* .

Manaal Faruqui and Chris Dyer. 2014. Improving vector space word representations using multilingual correlation. Association for Computational Linguistics.

Joseph Firth, John Torous, Jennifer Nicholas, Rebekah Carney, Simon Rosenbaum, and Jerome Sarris. 2017. Can smartphone mental health interventions reduce symptoms of anxiety? a meta-analysis of randomized controlled trials. *Journal of Affective Disorders* .

Seth Flaxman, Dino Sejdinovic, John P Cunningham, and Sarah Filippi. 2016. Bayesian learning of kernel embeddings. *arXiv preprint arXiv:1603.02160* .

Stephan Gouws, Yoshua Bengio, and Greg Corrado. 2015. Bilbowa: Fast bilingual distributed representations without word alignments. In *Proceedings of the 32nd International Conference on Machine Learning (ICML-15)*. pages 748–756.

David R Hardoon, Sandor Szedmak, and John Shawe-Taylor. 2004. Canonical correlation analysis: An overview with application to learning methods. *Neural computation* 16(12):2639–2664.

Felix Hill, Kyunghyun Cho, and Anna Korhonen. 2016. Learning distributed representations of sentences from unlabelled data. *arXiv preprint arXiv:1602.03483* .

Ryan Kiros, Yukun Zhu, Ruslan R Salakhutdinov, Richard Zemel, Raquel Urtasun, Antonio Torralba, and Sanja Fidler. 2015. Skip-thought vectors. In *Advances in neural information processing systems*. pages 3294–3302.

Dimitrios Kotzias, Misha Denil, Nando De Freitas, and Padhraic Smyth. 2015. From group to individual labels using deep features. In *Proceedings of the 21th ACM SIGKDD International Conference on Knowledge Discovery and Data Mining*. ACM, pages 597–606.

Erika B Litvin, Ana M Abrantes, and Richard A Brown. 2013. Computer and mobile technology-based interventions for substance use disorders: An organizing framework. *Addictive behaviors* 38(3):1747–1756.

Ang Lu, Weiran Wang, Mohit Bansal, Kevin Gimpel, and Karen Livescu. 2015. Deep multilingual correlation for improved word embeddings. In *HLT-NAACL*. pages 250–256.

Yong Luo, Jian Tang, Jun Yan, Chao Xu, and Zheng Chen. 2014. Pre-trained multi-view word embedding using two-side neural network. In *AAAI*. pages 1982–1988.

Siamak Mehrkanoon and Johan AK Suykens. 2017. Regularized semipaired kernel cca for domain adaptation. *IEEE Transactions on Neural Networks and Learning Systems* .

Tomas Mikolov, Ilya Sutskever, Kai Chen, Greg S Corrado, and Jeff Dean. 2013. Distributed representations of words and phrases and their compositionality. In *Advances in neural information processing systems*. pages 3111–3119.

John A Naslund, Lisa A Marsch, Gregory J McHugo, and Stephen J Bartels. 2015. Emerging mhealth and ehealth interventions for serious mental illness: a review of the literature. *Journal of mental health* 24(5):321–332.

Jeffrey Pennington, Richard Socher, and Christopher Manning. 2014. Glove: Global vectors for word representation. In *Proceedings of the 2014 conference on empirical methods in natural language processing (EMNLP)*. pages 1532–1543.

Andrew Quanbeck, Ming-Yuan Chih, Andrew Isham, Roberta Johnson, and David Gustafson. 2014. Mobile delivery of treatment for alcohol use disorders: A review of the literature. *Alcohol research: current reviews* 36(1):111.

Ali Sharif Razavian, Hossein Azizpour, Josephine Sullivan, and Stefan Carlsson. 2014. Cnn features off-the-shelf: an astounding baseline for recognition. In *Proceedings of the IEEE conference on computer vision and pattern recognition workshops*. pages 806–813.

Richard Socher, Alex Perelygin, Jean Wu, Jason Chuang, Christopher D Manning, Andrew Ng, and Christopher Potts. 2013. Recursive deep models for semantic compositionality over a sentiment treebank. In *Proceedings of the 2013 conference on empirical methods in natural language processing*. pages 1631–1642.

Yaniv Taigman, Ming Yang, Marc'Aurelio Ranzato, and Lior Wolf. 2014. Deepface: Closing the gap to human-level performance in face verification. In *Proceedings of the IEEE conference on computer vision and pattern recognition*. pages 1701–1708.

Chen-Tse Tsai and Dan Roth. 2016. Cross-lingual wikification using multilingual embeddings. In *HLT-NAACL*. pages 589–598.

Wenpeng Yin and Hinrich Schütze. 2016. Learning word meta-embeddings. In *Proceedings of the 54th Annual Meeting of the Association for Computational Linguistics (Volume 1: Long Papers)*. volume 1, pages 1351–1360.

Investigating Effective Parameters for Fine-tuning of Word Embeddings Using Only a Small Corpus

Kanako Komiya
Ibaraki University
4-12-1 Nakanarusawa
Hitachi Ibaraki 316-8511 Japan
`kanako.komiya.nlp@vc.`
`ibaraki.ac.jp`

Hiroyuki Shinnou
Ibaraki University
4-12-1 Nakanarusawa
Hitachi Ibaraki 316-8511 Japan
`hiroyuki.shinnou.0828@vc.`
`ibaraki.ac.jp`

Abstract

Fine-tuning is a popular method to achieve better performance when only a small target corpus is available. However, it requires tuning of a number of meta-parameters and thus it might carry risk of adverse effect when inappropriate meta-parameters are used. Therefore, we investigate effective parameters for fine-tuning when only a small target corpus is available. In the current study, we target at improving Japanese word embeddings created from a huge corpus. First, we demonstrate that even the word embeddings created from the huge corpus are affected by domain shift. After that, we investigate effective parameters for fine-tuning of the word embeddings using a small target corpus. We used perplexity of a language model obtained from a Long Short-Term Memory network to assess the word embeddings input into the network. The experiments revealed that fine-tuning sometimes give adverse effect when only a small target corpus is used and batch size is the most important parameter for fine-tuning. In addition, we confirmed that effect of fine-tuning is higher when size of a target corpus was larger.

1 Introduction

We investigate effective parameters for fine-tuning using nwjc2vec. Nwjc2vec is Japanese word2vec (the word embeddings proposed by (Mikolov et al., 2013)) created from NINJAL Web Japanese Corpus (NWJC) (Asahara et al., 2014) (Asahara and Teruaki, 2017). It contains 25.8 billion words as a whole. Therefore, it is believed that nwjc2vec is high-quality. In fact, some models used it showed better results (Yamaki et al., 2017) (Shinnou et al., 2017b) (Shinnou et al., 2017a). In addition, it is also believed that nwjc2vec is useful for various documents because it contains a number of documents described about various topics.

However, we show that a problem posed by domain shift occurs when nwjc2vec is used in the current study. (See Section 4)

The simplest and most effective approach to address the problem caused from domain shift of word embeddings is fine-tuning using a large target corpus. However, in practice, we often face the situation where only a small corpus of the target domain is available. It is possible to use other resources than a corpus, but they are not always available. Therefore, in the current study, we investigate effective parameters for word2vec, which is a program to create word embeddings, when we fine-tune nwjc2vec using only a small target corpus. (See Section 5)

We evaluate the word embeddings via language models obtained from a LSTM (Long Short-Term Memory) (Hochreiter and Schmidhuber, 1997) (Gers et al., 2000) (Greff et al., 2016) (See Section 3). First, we develop a language model using a LSTM. Usually, word embeddings are learned from the same corpus as a training corpus for a language model. In other words, when we have only a small target corpus, we use the word embeddings learned from the target corpus for the inputs for the LSTM that develops a language model. However, we input nwjc2vec fine-tuned using the small corpus into the LSTM instead of the word embeddings directly learned from the corpus. We evaluate the language model to assess the fine-tuned word embeddings assuming that the quality of the output language model is higher when the quality of the word embeddings used in the LSTM is higher.

Proceedings of the Workshop on Deep Learning Approaches for Low-Resource NLP, pages 60–67
Melbourne, Australia July 19, 2018. ©2018 Association for Computational Linguistics

The experiments revealed that the batch size is the most important parameter for word2vec to fine-tune nwjc2vec using a small corpus. In addition, they also showed that fine-tuning using inappropriate parameters sometimes make performance worse. Moreover, we confirmed that size of the corpus is crucial for fine-tuning. (See Sections 6 and 7)

2   Related Work

Generally, effectiveness of word embeddings depends on tasks and target domains of the tasks. Therefore, (Schnabel et al., 2015) proposed tuning of word embeddings according to tasks and their target domains.

The simplest tuning is fine-tuning, which is an approach where learned word embeddings are used for the initial values and tuned using an additional corpus. Its effectiveness has been shown for object recognition (Agrawal et al., 2014), named entity recognition (Lee et al., 2017), and many other tasks. Usually, a large target corpus is required for fine-tuning. Some works improved the word embeddings using external knowledges such as dictionaries. (Yu and Dredze, 2014) changed the loss function to use pre-knowledges and improved the word embeddings. (Faruqui et al., 2015) proposed to use retrofitting, which is an approach where the word embeddings obtained from a huge corpus are re-learned using external knowledges.

Fine-tuning is one of the methods for transfer learning (Pan and Yang, 2009). There are also much work about multi-task learning, which is another approach often used for transfer learning for neural networks (Aguilar et al., 2017) (von Däniken and Cieliebak, 2017).

3   Evaluation Method of Word Embeddings Using a LSTM

In the current study, we used a LSTM, which is an extended version of an a RNN to evaluate the word embeddings for a certain domain as (Shinnou et al., 2017a). We developed a language model using a LSTM from a training corpus and calculated the perplexity of the language model for a test corpus. Perplexity is given by the following equation.

$$PP = 2^H$$

where H is entropy given by the following equation.

$$H = \frac{1}{|D|} \sum_{i=1}^{|D|} -P(W_i|M)log_2 P(W_i|M)$$

where D denotes a size of test data, M denotes a language model, and W_i denotes i_{th} word in the test data.

We evaluate the quality of the word embeddings depending on the perplexity assuming that the quality of the output language model is higher when the quality of the word embeddings used in the LSTM is higher. Usually, word embeddings are learned from the same corpus as the training corpus for a language model. However, we used the word embeddings to be evaluated instead of the word embeddings learned together with the language model (cf. Figure1). We believe that we can evaluate the quality of the word embeddings by evaluating the perplexity of the language model when they are used in a LSTM.

4   Effect of Domain Shift for Nwjc2vec

We demonstrate that even nwjc2vec, which is a word embeddings obtained from a huge corpus, NWJC, has a problem posed by domain shift in this section.

4.1   Mai2Vec

To show this problem, we firstly created word embeddings from newspapers collected for seven years: Mainichi Shimbun newspaper articles from 1993 to 1999. We removed headlines and tables and extracted only sentences. The sentences were divided into words and the words were used for inputs into word2vec. The corpus had 6,791,403 sentences. We used MeCab-0.996 as a morphological analyzer and UniDic-2.1.2 as a dictionary. These word embeddings are referred to as mai2vec. The word2vec parameters used for mai2vec are the same as the parameters used for nwjc2vec. The final number of tokens of mai2vec we obtained was 132,509.

4.2   Language Model for Blogs and Q & A sites

First, we compared mai2vec with nwjc2vec using blogs and Q & A sites for test data. We extracted 7,330 sentences from blogs (Yahoo! blogs) and Q & A sites (Yahoo! Chiebukuro) of Balanced

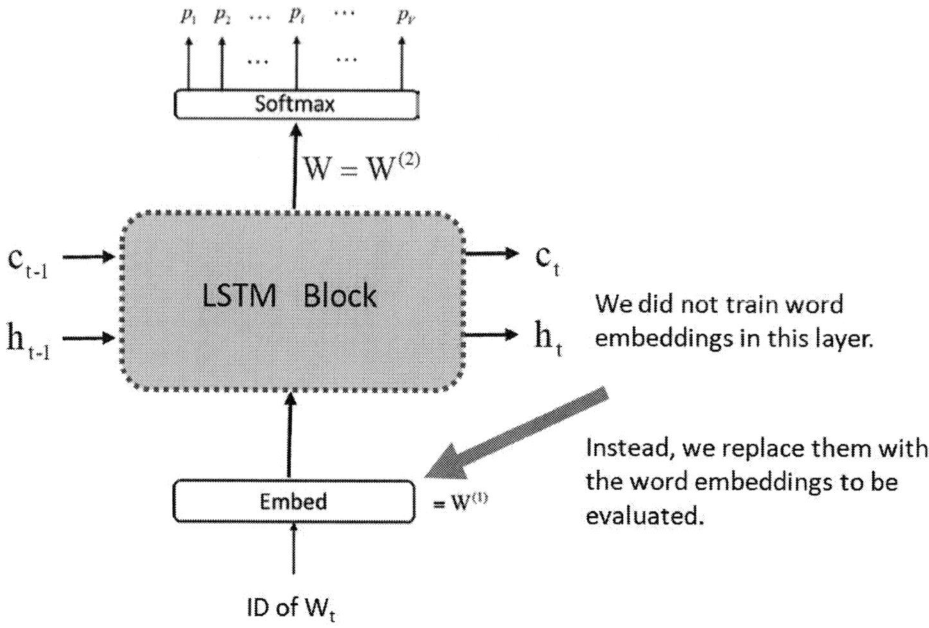

Figure 1: Evaluation Method of Word Embeddings Using LSTM

Corpora of Contemporary Witten Japanese (BC-CWJ) (Maekawa et al., 2014) and used them for the language model. We used 7,226 sentences for the training and 104 sentences for the test. The language model that used nwjc2vec in the LSTM was referred to as nwjc2vec-lm-1 and the language model that used mai2vec in the LSTM was referred to as mai2vec-lm-1. Base-lm-1, which was a language model that used the word embeddings learned together with the language model in the LSTM, was also evaluated for reference. Table 1 shows the corpora used for this experiment.

Perplexity was used for the evaluation of the language models. We conducted learning 15 epochs, saved the models, and calculated their perplexities for each epoch. After that, we evaluated the lowest perplexity for each model[1].

Table 2 shows the results. According to the table, the perplexity of nwjc2vec-lm-1 is the lowest, which indicates that the quality of nwjc2vec is higher than that of mai2vec.

However, the domains of the training and test corpora for the language model, blogs and Q &A site, were different from that of mai2vec, Mainichi Shimbun Newspaper. Therefore, nwjc2vec perhaps had an advantage.

4.3 Language Model for Newspaper

Next, we evaluate the word embeddings using the training and test corpora from newspapers, whose domain is the same as that of mai2vec. We used 100,000 sentences extracted from Mainichi Shimbun Newspaper in 2007 for the training of the language models. Ten thousand sentences extracted from Mainichi Shimbun Newspaper in 2008 were used for the test. Nwjc2vec-lm-2 and mai2vec-lm-2, which were the language models that used nwjc2vec and mai2vec respectively, were developed again. Base-lm-2, which was a language model that uses the word embeddings learned together with the language model in a LSTM, was also evaluated for reference. Note that the training corpora of word2vec for base-lm-1 and base-lm-2 are different. Table 3 shows the corpora used for this experiment.

Table 4 and Figure 2 show the results. They show that the perplexity of mai2vec-lm is the lowest, which indicates that the quality of mai2vec is higher than that of nwjc2vec.

The better method was shifted from nwjc2vec-lm into mai2vec-lm when the domain of the training and test corpora were the same as that of mai2vec. This fact indicates that even nwjc2vec has a problem posed by domain shift.

---

[1] The perplexity was the lowest at the fourth or fifth epoch for all the models.

Table 1: Corpora Used for Word2vec and Training and Test Data for Language Model for Blogs and Q & A Sites

Name of model	Word2Vec corpus	Training data	Test data
mai2vec-lm-1	Newspaper in from 1993 to 1999	Blogs	
nwjc2vec-lm-1	NWJC (Web pages)	And	
base-lm-1	Blogs and Q & A sites	Q & A sites	

Table 2: Evaluation of Language Models Obtained from Each Word Embeddings 1

base-lm-1	mai2vec-lm-1	nwjc2vec-lm-1
130.35	124.72	**118.68**

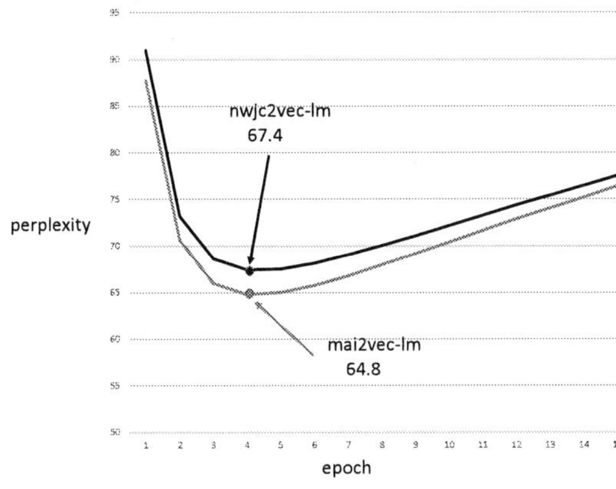

Figure 2: Perplexities of Language Models Developed Using Each Word Embeddings

Finally, Table 5 summarizes the number of sentences of each corpus. Please note that the corpora used for word2vec for base-lm-1 and base-lm-2 are the same as the corpora used for training the language models, respectively. The word embeddings were learned together with the LSTMs.

5 Fine-tuning Using a Small Corpus

Fine-tuning of nwjc2vec using a target corpus is the simplest way to address the problem caused from domain shift. It is preferable that the large target corpus is used for the fine-tuning but sometimes only a small target corpus is available. In these cases, it is not clear yet if the fine-tuning improves nwjc2vec.

Therefore, we tested various parameters of word2vec, which was a program to develop word embeddings, and found out if they were effective or not.

First, we set standard parameters of word2vec

and fine-tuned nwjc2vec through them using an additional corpus (the small target corpus). Next, only a windows size parameter was changed from the standard one and fine-tuned nwjc2vec through them using the same additional corpus. We changed the batch size and epoch number parameters and fine-tuned nwjc2vec in the same way.

Table 6 lists the standard parameters of word2vec for the fine-tuning.

The procedures to investigate the parameters are described as follows. First, we fine-tuned nwjc2vec using the standard parameters listed in Table 6 and developed word embeddings. The word embeddins developed in this setting are referred to as base_emb. Next, we changed the window size parameter into 8 and fine-tuned nwjc2vec. The word embeddins developed in this setting are referred to as win_emb. After that, we changed only the batch size parameter into 20 remaining the other parameters as the standard ones and fine-tuned nwjc2vec. The word embeddins developed in this setting are referred to as batch20_emb. We also evaluated batch100_emb, which were word embeddings fine-tuned using the standard parameters except the batch size, which had been changed into 100. Finally, we evaluated epch_emb, which were word embeddings fine-tuned using the standard parameters except the epoch number, which had been changed into 20. Table 7 lists the parameters of word2vec we tried for the fine-tuning. We tested the five settings of fine-tuning including the setting in Table 6. We used 100,000 sentences randomly extracted from Mainichi Shimbun in from 1993 to 1999 as an additional corpus for the fine-tuning.

6 Experiments

We developed the language models through the LSTMs. We used the five fine-tuned word embeddings described above, base_emb, win_emb, batch20_emb, batch100_emb, and epch_emb, and used 100,000 sentences randomly extracted from Mainichi Shimbun Newspaper in from 1993 to

Table 3: Corpora Used for Word2vec and Training and Test Data for Language Model for Newspapers

Name of model	Word2Vec corpora	Training data	Test data
mai2vec-lm-2	Newspaper in from 1993 to 1999	Newspaper In	Newspaper In
nwjc2vec-lm-2	NWJC (Web pages)		
base-lm-2	Newspaper in 2007	2007	2008

Table 4: Evaluation of Language Models Obtained from Each Word Embeddings 2

base-lm-2	mai2vec-lm-2	nwjc2vec-lm-2
81.52	**64.81**	67.47

1999 to train the LSTMs. We calculated perplexities of the language models obtained from the LSTMs at each epoch using the test data, which was 10,000 sentences from the same corpus as the training data. These is no overlap among the data for the fine-tuning, the training, and the testing. Table 8 summarizes the number of sentences of each corpus.

Table 9 and Figure 3 show the results. They include the perplexities of the language model obtained from the LSTMs when original nwjc2vec was used without the fine-tuning. The asterisks in the table mean that the language model using the fine-tuned word embeddings was better than that using nwjc2vec.

parameters are used in the case where small corpora are used.

7　Discussion

We think that although we might obtain better performance if we changed parameters other than batch size, the best results would be around the performance of batch100_emb because the batch size affected much more than the window size and the epoch number according to Table 9 and Figure 3.

In addition, we believe that the most important factor for the effective fine-tuning of nwjc2vec is the size of the additional corpus. To confirm this point, we tried some variation of the additional corpus size, 200,000 and 300,000 sentences in addition to the original setting, 100,000 sentences.

Table 10 and Figure 4 list the results of these experiments. These results indicate that the effect of fine-tuning is higher when the size of the additional corpus is larger.

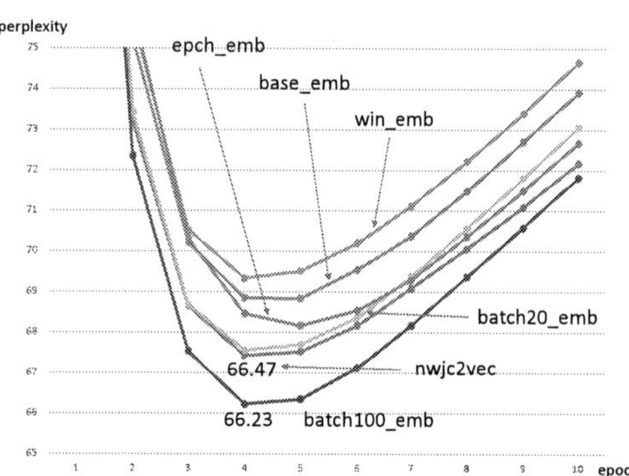

Figure 3: Changes of Perplexities According to Various Settings

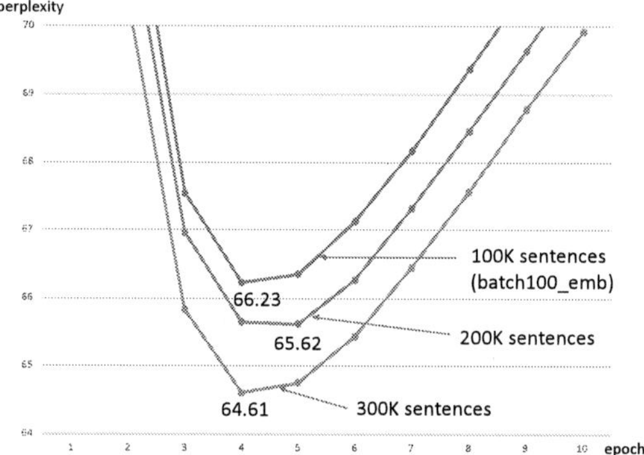

Figure 4: Changes of Perplexities According to Various Sizes of Additional Corpora

These results show that the perplexities of the language model decrease only when batch100_emb is used. It indicates that fine-tuning is only effective when the batch size parameter is changed into 100. Other parameter changes made the results worse. The experiments revealed that fine-tuning has an opposite effect when unsuitable

The fine-tuning approach we employed is the simplest way to tune word embeddings. Fine tuning of nwjc2vec requires large-sized additional corpus. Instead of the additional corpus, the external resources such as dictionaries would be useful. We plan to improve nwjc2vec using such external resources in the future.

Table 5: Corpus Data for Domain Shift Experiments

Corpus	Type	Aim	Genre	Number of Sentences
NWJC	Training	Nwjc2vec	Web pages	1,463,142,939
Mainichi Shimbun 1993-1999	Training	Mai2vec	Newspaper	6,791,403
BCCWJ	Training	Word2vec of base-lm-1	Blogs	7,226
		Language model	And	
BCCWJ	Test	For blogs and Q &A sites	Q & A sites	104
Mainichi Shimbun 2007	Training	Word2vec of base-lm-2		100,000
		Language model	Newspaper	
Mainichi Shimbun 2008	Test	For newspaper		10,000

Table 6: Standard Parameters for Word2vec

Model Name	base_emb
Number of Units	200
Window Size	5
Batch Size	10
Epoch Number	10
Used Model	skip-gram

8 Conclusion

We showed the problem occurred by domain shift when nwjc2vec was used and investigated the effective parameters of word2vec to fine-tune nwjc2vec using a small corpus.

The experiments revealed that it is possible to obtain better results using fine-tuning of nwjc2vec if we properly adjust parameters. We showed that the most effective parameter of the fine-tuning is the batch size and fine-tuning using improper parameters make the results worse. Finally, we demonstrated that the size of the additional corpus is crucial for fine-tuning of nwjc2vec. We plan to use external resources instead of the large-sized corpus in the future.

References

Pulkit Agrawal, Ross Girshick, and Jitendra Malik. 2014. Analyzing the Performance of Multilayer Neural Networks for Object Recognition. In *Proceedings of ECCV-2014*, page arXiv:1407.1610.

Gustavo Aguilar, Suraj Maharjan, A. Pastor Lopez-Monroy, and Thamar Solorio. 2017. A Multi-task Approach for Named Entity Recognition in Social Media Data. In *Proceedings of the 3rd Workshop on Noisy User-generated Text*, pages 148–153.

Masayuki Asahara, Kikuo Maekawa, Mizuho Imada, Sachi Kato, and Hikari Konishi. 2014. Archiving and Analysing Techniques of the Ultra-large-scale Web-based Corpus Project of NINJAL, Japan. *Alexandria: The Journal of National and International Library and Information Issues*, 25(1-2):129–148.

Masayuki Asahara and Oka Teruaki. 2017. nwjc2vec: word embedding data based on NINJAL Japanese Web Corpus (in Japanese). In *ANLP-2017*, pages 94–97.

Pius von Däniken and Mark Cieliebak. 2017. Transfer Learning and Sentence Level Features for Named Entity Recognition on Tweets. In *Proceedings of the 3rd Workshop on Noisy User-generated Text*, pages 166–171.

Manaal Faruqui, Jesse Dodge, Sujay K. Jauhar, Chris Dyer, Eduard Hovy, and Noah A. Smith. 2015. Retrofitting Word Vectors to Semantic Lexicons. In *Proceedings of NAACL*.

Felix A Gers, Jürgen Schmidhuber, and Fred Cummins. 2000. Learning to forget: Continual prediction with LSTM. *Neural computation*, 12(10):2451–2471.

Klaus Greff, Rupesh Kumar Srivastava, Jan Koutník, Bas R Steunebrink, and Jürgen Schmidhuber. 2016. LSTM: A Search Space Odyssey. *IEEE transactions on neural networks and learning systems*.

Sepp Hochreiter and Jürgen Schmidhuber. 1997. Long short-term memory. *Neural Computation*, 9(8):1735–1780.

Ji Young Lee, Franck Dernoncourt, and Peter Szolovits. 2017. Transfer Learning for Named-Entity Recognition with Neural Networks. In *arXiv*, page arXiv:1705.06273.

Kikuo Maekawa, Makoto Yamazaki, Toshinobu Ogiso, Takehiko Maruyama, Hideki Ogura, Wakako Kashino, Hanae Koiso, Masaya Yamaguchi, Makiro Tanaka, and Yasuharu Den. 2014. Balanced corpus of contemporary written japanese. *Language Resources and Evaluation*, 48(2):345–371.

Tomas Mikolov, Ilya Sutskever, Kai Chen, Greg S Corrado, and Jeff Dean. 2013. Distributed representations of words and phrases and their compositionality. In *Advances in neural information processing systems*, pages 3111–3119.

Table 7: Standard Parameters for Word2vec

Model Names	win_emb	batch20_emb	batch100_emb	epoch_emb
Number of Units	200			
Window Size	8	5	5	5
Batch Size	10	20	100	10
Epoch Number	10	10	10	20
Used Model	skip-gram			

Table 8: Corpus Data for Fine-tuning Experiments

Corpus	Type	Aim	Genre	Number of Sentences
Mainichi Shimbun	Fine-tuning	Word2vec		100,000
1993-	Training	Language	Newspaper	100,000
1999	Test	Model		10,000

Sinno Jialin Pan and Qiang Yang. 2009. A survey on transfer learning. *IEEE TRANSACTIONS ON KNOWLEDGE AND DATA ENGINEERING*, 22(10):1345 – 1359.

Tobias Schnabel, Igor Labutov, David M Mimno, and Thorsten Joachims. 2015. Evaluation methods for unsupervised word embeddings. In *EMNLP 2015*, pages 298–307.

Hiroyuki Shinnou, Masayuki Asahara, Kanako Komiya, and Minoru Sasaki. 2017a. nwjc2vec: Word Embedding Data Constructed from NINJAL Web Japanese Corpus. *Journal of Natural Language Processing*, 24(5):705–720.

Hiroyuki Shinnou, Kanako Komiya, and Minoru Sasaki. 2017b. Supervised Word Sense Disambiguation using Forward Multilayered LSTM and Word Embeddings (in Japanese). In *IPSJ Natural Language Processing Report*, pages NL–232–4.

Shoma Yamaki, Hiroyuki Shinnou, Kanako Komiya, and Minoru Sasaki. 2017. Construction of word embeddings using labeled data (in Japanese). In *ANLP-2017*, pages 78–81.

Mo Yu and Mark Dredze. 2014. Improving Lexical Embeddings with Semantic Knowledge. In *ACL (2)*, pages 545–550.

Table 9: Perplexities of Various Settings

epoch	nwjc2vec	base_emb	win_emb	batch20_emb	batch100_emb	epch_emb
1	91.03	93.70	95.36	91.51	89.69	95.06
2	73.20	75.21	75.71	73.43	72.36	75.89
3	68.65	70.21	70.52	68.69	67.54	70.30
4	**67.43**	68.85	**69.33**	**67.56**	**66.23***	68.46
5	67.52	**68.84**	69.51	67.70	66.35*	**68.17**
6	68.17	69.55	70.20	68.37	67.13*	68.54
7	69.08	70.37	71.11	69.37	68.17	69.29
8	70.06	71.48	72.22	70.56	69.37	70.36
9	71.09	72.71	73.40	71.80	70.58	71.49
10	72.18	73.92	74.66	73.06	71.82	72.68

Table 10: Perplexities of Sizes of Additional Corpora

epoch	100 thousand sentences (batch100_emb)	200 thousand sentences	300 thousand sentences
1	89.69	89.55	87.94
2	72.36	71.50	70.28
3	67.54	66.96	65.83
4	**66.23**	65.65	**64.61**
5	66.35	**65.62**	64.75
6	67.13	66.27	65.44
7	68.17	67.32	66.45
8	69.37	68.46	67.56
9	70.58	69.64	68.78
10	71.82	70.89	69.92

Semi-Supervised Learning with Auxiliary Evaluation Component for Large Scale e-Commerce Text Classification

Mingkuan Liu, Musen Wen, Selcuk Kopru, Xianjing Liu, Alan Lu
eBay Inc.,
2145 Hamilton Avenue, San Jose, CA, 95032, USA
{mingkliu,mwen,skopru,xianjliu,alalu}@ebay.com

Abstract

The lack of high-quality labeled training data has been one of the critical challenges facing many industrial machine learning tasks. To tackle this challenge, in this paper, we propose a semi-supervised learning method to utilize unlabeled data and user feedback signals to improve the performance of ML models. The method employs a primary model $Main$ and an auxiliary evaluation model $Eval$, where $Main$ and $Eval$ models are trained iteratively by automatically generating labeled data from unlabeled data and/or users feedback signals. The proposed approach is applied to different text classification tasks. We report results on both the publicly available Yahoo! Answers dataset and our e-commerce product classification dataset. The experimental results show that the proposed method reduces the classification error rate by 4% and up to 15% across various experimental setups and datasets. A detailed comparison with other semi-supervised learning approaches is also presented later in the paper. The results from various text classification tasks demonstrate that our method outperforms those developed in previous related studies.

1 Introduction

There are many ways to improve the performance of a machine learning model. Improving the training data is one such method. Obtaining high-quality training data, such as human labeled data, is usually expensive and time-consuming. Many machine learning systems use unlabeled data or a mixture of labeled and unlabeled data for training because it is cheaper and easier to collect enormous amounts of unlabeled data. Industry-deployed machine learning systems that serve millions of users generate vast amounts of unlabeled data and noisy user feedback signals every day. Those data and signals are very important and can be utilized in the training of real-world machine learning systems.

In this paper, we propose a new semi-supervised learning method with a feedback loop to leverage vast amounts of unlabeled data and feedback signals. In particular, we train two machine learning models iteratively. The main model, which is represented as $Main$, performs the main task at runtime. The auxiliary model, which is represented as $Eval$, works offline and it estimates the correctness of the $Main$ models output. The information available to the auxiliary model $Eval$ is much richer than the run-time model $Main$. Extra data, such as user feed-back data and session context information, can be used when training the auxiliary model. The idea is to control the false positive rate of $Eval$ to produce high-quality, automatically labeled data from unlabeled data. The entire process runs iteratively and the performance of both models is improved in an iterative manner. The assumption of run-time $Main$ model has much fewer available information is due to the business logic flow and/or UX design constraints which limit the run-time $Main$ model to collect richer features in some industry setups.

In this paper, we use text classification experiments to illustrate the proposed approach. However, this semi-supervised learning approach can also be applied to other machine learning tasks, such as machine translation and search relevance.

Different semi-supervised learning approaches have been previously proposed to leverage unlabeled data, including Blum and Mitchell (1998), Weiss et al. (2016), Goodfellow et al. (2014) and

Proceedings of the Workshop on Deep Learning Approaches for Low-Resource NLP, pages 68–76
Melbourne, Australia July 19, 2018. ©2018 Association for Computational Linguistics

Cohn et al. (1996). Experimental results on the public Yahoo! Answers dataset and on a new public e-commerce dataset for product classification demonstrate the advantages and potential of the proposed framework compared with previous work.

The contributions of this work are as follows:

- A new semi-supervised learning method with the introducing of an auxiliary evaluation component, and

- A scalable, cost-effective and efficient way to convert vast amounts of unlabeled data into high quality labeled data for supervised training purposes.

In section 2, we present the details of the proposed semi-supervised learning approach in the context of text classification tasks. In section 3, the theoretical analysis of the proposed method is provided. Next, we give an overview of related works and highlight their differences compared to our approach. Section 5 defines various experimental setups and presents the results for two different datasets. Finally, we present the papers conclusions in section 6.

2 Proposed Method

2.1 Modeling Approach

The suggested method is based on a few observations from real-world machine learning systems.

- The main model $Main$ that serves online users may have limited information available at prediction time due to the business logic flow or UX design constraints in industry setups. Therefore, the predictions from the $Main$ component may contain errors and cannot be used directly as labeled data for model training purposes.

- The evaluation model $Eval$ runs offline. Hence, it can access much richer information than the main task component without those constraints. User feedback data, user behavioral data, prior and post task session history data, and the knowledge base about the users main task constitute richer offline information. All those data helps the $Eval$ model to reliably estimate whether Mains output is acceptable or not.

- Large-scale supervised machine learning methods typically need a larger amount of labeled training data for a good performance. However, in reality, it is very expensive to manually label millions of training data. On the other hand, large scale machine learning systems serving millions of users are generating millions of unlabeled data and user feedback signals every day that is not effectively utilized.

The main idea of the proposed approach is to train and deploy two parallel machine learning models. The first model $Main$ is used to serve live user requests for the main task. The second machine learning model $Eval$ is used as an offline model to estimate the accuracy of $Mains$ prediction. The $Eval$ model utilizes additional signals, such as user feedback signals, system logs that are related to user sessions, the output confidence scores from Main, etc. An EM-style iterative process is applied to train $Main$ and $Eval$ in a repeated manner. High-quality, automatically labeled data are extracted from unlabeled data by controlling the false positive rate and the false negative rate in $Eval$. Mathematical analysis (section 3) and experiments (section 5) on different datasets show that after multiple iterations, the accuracy of Main can be improved substantially.

Algorithm 1 shows the details of the proposed semi-supervised learning algorithm. The input to the algorithm is an initial small set of labeled data L, a large set of unlabeled data U and an optional set of user feedback data F. The algorithm leverages the auxiliary evaluation model $Eval$ and the optional user feedback data F to produce high-quality, automatically labeled data AL from a large amount of unlabeled data U. Once the labeled data AL is extracted and added to the training corpus C, we use a shallow neural network[1] to train model $Main$ for the text classification tasks.

2.2 Auxiliary Evaluation Model

The auxiliary evaluation model $Eval$ is a binary classifier that predicts whether the automatic label is correct or not. It is trained using gradient boosting[2]. If the false positive rate of the eval-

---

[1] We use the FastText library Joulin et al. (2016) for the shallow neural network implementation.

[2] We use the XGboost library Chen and Guestrin (2016) for gradient boosting.

Algorithm 1 Proposed Algorithm

Given:
Labeled dataset $L : \{l_i\}$
Unlabeled dataset $U : \{u_i\}$
Optional feedback data $F : \{f_i\}$
$Main$ = trainMainModel(L)
$fpRate$ = false positive rate threshold
for $k = 1$ **to** $MaxIter$ **do**
  $Eval$ = trainEvalModel($Main$, L, F)
  AL = emptyList()
  for u_i **in** U **do**
    PC_i = predClass(M, u_i)
    $Score(PC_i)$ = evalScore(E, u_i, f_i, PC_i)
    if $Score(PC_i) > (1 - fpRate)$ **then**
      AL.append(u_i, PC_i)
    end if
  end for
  $C = L + AL$
  M = trainMainModel(C)
end for

---

uation model $Eval$ is controlled at a low threshold, vast amounts of high-quality, automatically labeled data can be extracted from the unlabeled data.

For text classification tasks, the evaluation model $Eval$ leverages a variety of features. The confidence score of the main model $Main$s prediction, the n-gram language model related ranking, the input sentence probability scores evaluated by the language model from $Main$s predicted class and the optional noisy user feedback signal about $Main$s output are the features used by $Eval$. The language model related ranking and input sentence probability scores are based on the assumption that sentences belonging to the same class are more similar than sentences belonging to different classes. Thus, we train a language model SLM_i for each $CLASS_i$ using sentences belonging to that class. If a sentence belongs to $CLASS_i$, its sentence probability that is evaluated with SLM_i should be higher than the sentence probability evaluated with $CLASS_j$, where $i \neq j$. We use the trigram statistical language model[3] to train SLM_i for each $CLASS_i$.

Details on how to train the auxiliary evaluation model $Eval$ are described in Algorithm 2. The input to the algorithm is the $Main$ model, the labeled data L and the optional set of user feedback

---

[3]We use KenLM library Heafield (2011) to build and query SLMs.

---

data F. For each example in L, based on l_is labeled class, we create one positive training sample with the correct class and one negative training sample with a wrong class that is chosen randomly. The features can be generated using the aforementioned multiple signal sources, such as Ms prediction confidence scores, the SLM ranking scores and the optional user feedback.

Algorithm 2 Train Auxiliary Evaluation Model

Given:
$Main$ model
Labeled data $L : \{l_i\}$
Optional feedback data $F : \{f_i\}$
for l_j **in** L **do**
  $CLASS_i$ = class label of l_j
  Append l_j to $SLMCorpus_i$
end for
for i **in** $AllClasses$ **do**
  SLM_i = trainSLM($SLMCorpus_i$)
end for
$Corpus_{xgb}$ = emptyList()
for l_j **in** L **do**
  $CLASS_i$ = class label of l_j
  $XgbSample_+$ = getXgbFeatures(l_j,f_j, M, $SLMs$, $CLASS_i$)
  $XgbSample_-$ = getXgbFeatures(l_j,f_j, M, $SLMs$, $CLASS_k$ where $k \neq i$)
  $Corpus_{xgb}$.append($+$, $XgbSample_+$)
  $Corpus_{xgb}$.append($-$, $XgbSample_-$)
end for
$Eval$ = trainXgbModel($Corpus_{xgb}$)

---

3 Theoretical Analysis

The EM-like semi-supervised learning approach with an auxiliary evaluation component is designed to tackle large scale ML problems. In section 5, we will demonstrate that our framework has a superior and consistently better performance in various real-world machine learning tasks based on the empirical results. In this section, we will first analyze and highlight some mathematical aspects of this dual-player, semi-supervised learning approach, and illustrate its deep connection to the Expectation-Maximization algorithm.

Suppose we are given an initial set of N manually labeled text $S^{(0)}$, and our main task is to classify unseen text to a label. As described before, we use a shallow neural network similar to Joulin et al. (2016) to build the $Main$ model. For this purpose, according to Joulin et al. (2016), we want to minimize the negative log-likelihood

$$-\frac{1}{N}\sum_{1}^{N} y_n log\left(f\left(BAx_n\right)\right) \tag{1}$$

where x_n is the normalized bag of features of the nth text, y_n is the category labels, and A and B are the weight matrices. As part of the auxiliary evaluation component $Eval$, we established a machine learning system with richer context compared to $Main$. The task of $Eval$ is to estimate the probability that the given input text belongs to the category predicted by $Main$. This probability is defined as p_{text_i,c_j}.

$$p_{text_i,c_j} = P(C_j|text_i) \tag{2}$$

Notice that the entire purpose of the evaluation system is to select newly labeled data to enrich the training set of the main machine learning system. Thus, the $Eval$ model estimates the confidence score of this prediction for each sample. The whole learning process of $Main \rightarrow Eval$ iterates as described in the previous sections. The dual system runs iteratively. We stress that it has a close connection to the popular Expectation-Maximization algorithm Dempster et al. (1977) via the following result.

Theory 1. *Given a two-player machine learning system comprised of Main and Eval, the Main model converges to the local minima of the negative log-likelihood with the controlled false positive rate given enough capacity.*

Proof. Given a set of training data $\mathcal{S}^{(0)} = (\mathbf{x}_i, y_i)$, $i = 1, \cdots, N$, which are the observed features and labels, let us denote a hidden variable $z_i \in \{0, 1\}$ that is a variable indicating the quality of the observation. z_i takes a value of 1 if the label for the corresponding instance is correct or relevant, and 0 otherwise. Without the loss of generality, suppose that the $Main$ model is trained to maximize the log-likelihood function:

$$\ell(\Theta|\mathbf{X}, \mathbf{Y}) \tag{3}$$

Using equation (1), equation (3) can be rewritten as

$$
\begin{aligned}
\ell(\Theta|\mathbf{X}, \mathbf{Y}) &= \log p(\mathbf{X}, \mathbf{Y}|\Theta) \\
&= \log \sum_z p(\mathbf{x}, y, z|\Theta) \\
&= \log \sum_z p(z)\frac{p(\mathbf{x}, y, z|\Theta)}{p(z)} \\
&\geq \sum_z p(z) \log \frac{p(\mathbf{x}, y, z|\Theta)}{p(z)} \\
&= \mathbf{E}_{p(z)} \log p(p(\mathbf{x}, y, z|\Theta) \\
&\quad + Entropy[p(z)] \\
&= L(p, \Theta; \mathbf{X}, \mathbf{Y})
\end{aligned}
\tag{4}
$$

where the inequality is obtained by Jensen's inequality. The equality holds if and only if

$$p(z) = p(z|\mathbf{X}, y, \Theta)$$

The term $\mathbf{E}_{p(z)} \log p(p(\mathbf{x}, y, z|\Theta)$ is the expected complete log-likelihood (or, **Q-function**). The two machine learning systems then iterate through the following two steps. From a set of noisy data, $Eval$ performs similarly in the **E-step** of the EM algorithm. For n^{th} step, ($n = 1, 2, \cdots$):

$$
\begin{aligned}
p(z)^{(n)} &= \arg\max_p L\left(p, \Theta^{(n-1)}; \mathbf{X}, \mathbf{Y}\right) \\
&= p(z|\mathbf{X}, y, \Theta^{(n-1)})
\end{aligned}
\tag{5}
$$

Notice that the conditional distribution of the hidden variable z is not necessarily fully predictable by the machine learning model even if the observed data and the models parameters are given. The evaluation system mainly provides a confidence score of the correctness or confidence of the prediction, which is defined by equation (5). By properly controlling the false positive rate, we select only those new training examples with a good estimate of $p(z)^{(n)}$ by the $Eval$ model. This results in a set of filtered samples $\mathcal{S}^{(n)}$ to be added to our $Main$ system for the next iteration. The main system then performs the maximization step role in the EM algorithm framework, which is the M-step that follows:

$$
\begin{aligned}
\Theta^{(n+1)} &= \arg\max_\Theta L\left(p^{(n)}, \Theta; \mathbf{X}, \mathbf{Y}\right) \\
&= \arg\max_\Theta \mathbf{E}_{p(z)^{(n)}} \log p(\mathbf{x}, y, z|\Theta)
\end{aligned}
\tag{6}
$$

over $\mathcal{S}^{(0)} \cup \mathcal{S}^{(1)} \cup \cdots \cup \mathcal{S}^{(n)}$ which is readily solvable from the main machine learning system. Notice that in the **M-step**, it is not necessary to find the optimal values over the whole parameter space. Using the monotonic convergence property of the generalized EM algorithm, given enough capacity, the $Main$ system would eventually converge to its local optimum after enough iterations. □

In the e-commerce scenario, we have more informative features in the offline $Eval$ system, and thus the evaluation system can have a very high accuracy. According to the proof, the main machine learning system eventually reaches a stable state.

4 Related Work

Various semi-supervised learning approaches have been proposed to leverage unsupervised data to improve the performance of machine learning systems Triguero et al. (2015).

Active learning Cohn et al. (1996); Nigam et al. (1998); Beygelzimer et al. (2009), which is a special kind of semi-supervised learning, provides ways to actively select the most informative data samples from a vast amount of unlabeled data. The selected samples are then labeled by humans. In this way, the total amount of data needed for manual labeling is reduced to save resources. How to handle the problem of label quality is one of the active areas of active learning research. Zhang and Chaudhuri (2015) studied the problem of active learning where labels were obtained from strong and weak labelers. In addition to the standard active learning setting, they consider the problem where they have extra weaker labelers that may provide incorrect labels. Yan et al. (2016) studies the adaptive active learning problem where the labeler can return incorrect labels and also abstain from labeling.

Although active learning can significantly reduce the amount of manual labeling, it still requires extra human labeling, which is costly and time consuming. Compared with active learning, our approach does not require any additional manual labeling effort.

The self-labeled technique is another type of semi-supervised approach to boost the models performance by iteratively labeling parts of the unlabeled data. This approach aims to obtain an enlarged labeled set, which is based on its most confident predictions, to classify unlabeled data. Zhu and Goldberg (2009) divides the self-labeled methods into self-training and co-training.

In the self-training process Triguero et al. (2014); Yarowsky (1995), a model is trained with an initially small number of human labeled examples that aim to predict unlabeled data. Then, it is retrained with its most confident predictions, thus enlarging its labeled training set. The process iterates in the same manner.

In the co-training process Blum and Mitchell (1998); Chen et al. (2011), two learning models are trained separately to provide distinct views of the data set by using different feature sets of the data. These two models are initially trained with a small amount of human labeled data, and then the most confident predictions of one model on the unlabeled data are used to construct the training data for the other model. This process is repeated iteratively. Similar to our proposed approach, the self-labeled method uses the EM-based iterative process to boost the models accuracy and also does not need any further manual labeling efforts.

The major difference between the self-labeled approach and our approach is as follows. In the self-labeled method, with either self-training or co-training, all the models are main task machine learning models. In our proposed approach, there exists only one main-task model and another auxiliary evaluation model that runs offline. Using an offline auxiliary evaluation model has the benefit of utilizing offline information that is not available at prediction time. Thus, the auxiliary evaluation model has a better estimation capability than the main model regarding whether Mains output is correct or not.

The Generative Adversarial Network Goodfellow et al. (2014) is another semi-supervised approach that tries to generate unlimited synthetic fake samples that can mimic real data. The GAN also builds two models, namely, the generative model and the discriminative model, and puts them against each other. The generative model takes random inputs and tries to generate output data that looks similar to real data. The discriminative model takes input data from both the generative model and real data and tries to correctly distinguish between them. The GAN has been successfully applied to image and audio areas where the synthetic data is real-valued. It's quite challenging for the GAN to generate sequence of discrete tokens in the NLP domain. Yu et al. (2017) has proposed the SeqGAN method to address this challenge by directly performing gradient policy update with reinforcement learning. Kusner and Hernández-Lobato (2016) proposed an alternative method to address this challenge using the Gumbel-softmax distribution.

One of the differences between our approach and GAN is that our approach relies on real unlabeled data while the GAN generates plausible data with random inputs. Another major difference is that the evaluation component in our approach tries to evaluate whether the main model results are correct or not. Meanwhile, in the GAN approach, the adversarial component learns to tell whether the current data sample is real or fake.

5 Experiments

To illustrate the effectiveness of the proposed semi-supervised learning method, we evaluate it with different text classification tasks. We compare the new method with a few other benchmark semi-supervised approaches using the public Yahoo! Answers topic classification dataset Zhang et al. (2015); Joulin et al. (2016) and our e-commerce product categorization dataset.

5.1 Yahoo! Answers Dataset Experiments

The Yahoo! Answers topic classification dataset contains 10 classes. Each class contains 140K training samples and 6K testing samples. In this dataset, the total number of training instances is 1.4M and total number of test instances is 60K Zhang et al. (2015). We shuffle and split the original 1.4 M labeled training data into two sets. The first set contains 100K instances with labels and is used as the initial labeled dataset L. The second set contains 1.3 M instances and the labels are deleted to form the unlabeled dataset U. The 60K test samples are untouched as the blind test set T.

5.1.1 Results

Using the initial 100K labeled dataset L and 1.3 M unlabeled dataset U, we compare our approach to the three benchmark approaches: supervised learning, co-training and active-learning. In all experiments, once the labeled training corpus for the main model is derived, we use the shallow neural network classifier described in Joulin et al. (2016) to train $Main$.

1. **1.4M Supervised Learning:** Use the entire Yahoo! dataset and build a model similar to Joulin et al. (2016). The accuracy is reported as 72.3%. This is the theoretical upper bound for a semi-supervised learning training. Any pro-

posed method with less labeled data tries approach this accuracy.

2. **100K Supervised Learning:** Use L dataset and build a model similar to Joulin et al. (2016). The accuracy for this model is 65.9%. This is the lower bound result. Any proposed method to leverage unlabeled data should outperform this number as much as possible.

3. **Co-Training:** Use L to build two initial models and use U data in a co-training setup to enhance the initial models. The system converged to an accuracy of 69.03% after 40 iterations.

4. **Self-Training:** Use L to train an initial model and use this initial model to predict the labels of U. In the next step, mix L and U with its predictions to train a new model. Keep iterating the predicting labels for U, mixing corpus and training the classifier until the system converges. In our experiments, the self-labeled baseline converged after 30 iterations to an accuracy of 67.5%.

5. **Active Learning:** Train the initial classifier L, use it to evaluate and select the most informative samples from U and reveal their ground truth labels. Then, update the classifier with the mixed corpus of L and reveal the label samples. As more samples get selected, the performance of the active-learning algorithm improves. Fig 1 shows the improvements in the accuracy with the increasing amount of manual labeling data.

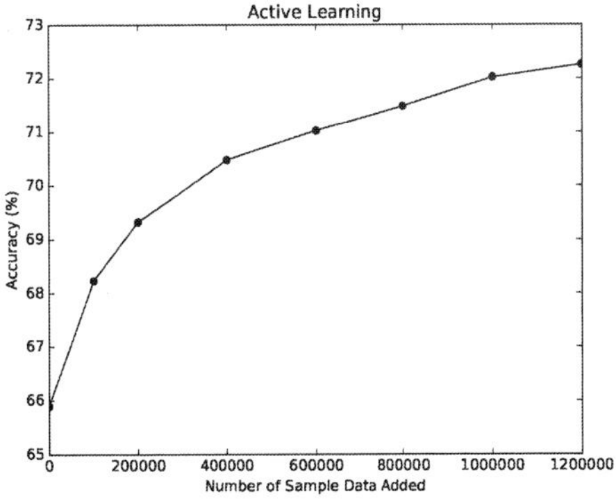

Figure 1: active learning accuracy w.r.t the number of samples selected for labeling

6. **EMAEC without Enriched Data:** Use L and U and apply Algorithm 1 and Algorithm 2 to iteratively train $Main$ and $Eval$. After approximately 20 iterations, $Main$ can achieve an accuracy of 70.42%. The $Eval$ model yields 92.8% precision with 83.5% recall. At the convergence stage, the system generated labels for 1.12M instances in U with a false positive rate of $<8\%$. This approach automatically labels the majority ($>86\%$) of the U dataset with high-quality (error rate $<8\%$).

7. **EMAEC with Enriched Data:** The Yahoo! dataset does not contain any additional user session feedback data. To simulate the scenario where user-provided feedback data is unreliable to produce 100% correct automatic labels, we assume that user feedback data can be simulated by randomly introducing noises to the original ground truth labels in the dataset. Thus, we first reveal all the ground truth labels in U, and then randomly select $x\%$ of U. Next, we randomly flip their correct labels into wrong labels and then mix them with the remaining instances in U. We call the mixed and blurred dataset as B which is the U dataset with noisy labels. We use the B dataset to simulate user noisy feedback signals. In this experiment, we use L, B, Algorithm 1 and Algorithm 2 to iteratively train $Main$ and $Eval$. As expected, the higher that the level of blurring is, the worse that the system performs. The theoretical upper bound for this experiment would be a classifier trained with 100K + $(1 - x\%)$ * 1.3M ground truth labeled data. Figure 2 demonstrates the varying system performance varying with different noise level $x\%$. We can see that user feedback loop data can further improve the system's performance even if we introduce 50% noise to B.

5.1.2 Discussion

The experimental results on the Yahoo! Answers topic classification dataset are summarized in Table 1. The results demonstrate that by starting with only 100K labeled data and 1.3 M unlabeled data, and by using an auxiliary evaluation component, the systems accuracy can be increased from 65.9% to 70.4%. Active learning can reach the same performance only after adding another 400K manually labeled data.

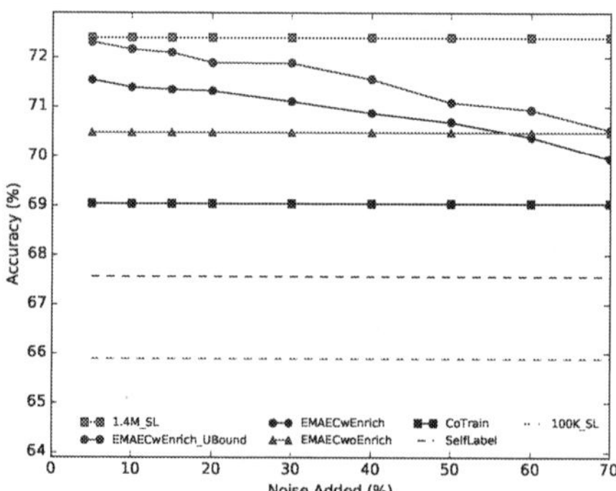

Figure 2: EMAEC with enriched data at different noise levels and the comparison with other baselines.

Approach	Accuracy [%]	Error Reduction [%]
100K Supervised Learning	65.90	0.000
Self-Training	67.57	4.888
Active Learning (extra 100K labeled)	68.23	6.85
Co-Training	69.04	9.208
Active Learning (extra 400K labeled)	70.48	13.436
EMAEC w/o Enriched Data	**70.49**	**13.456**
EMAEC w/ Enriched Data (20% noise)	**71.33**	**15.913**
Supervised Learning with 20% noise	57.8	-12.29
1.4M Supervised Learning	72.40	19.062

Table 1: Test accuracy and error reduction rate [%] on the Yahoo! Answers dataset. The method proposed in this study is printed in bold.

Moreover, the proposed approach can automatically generate high-quality labels for over 86% of the unlabeled data with an error rate less than 8%.

The results also show that by adding simulated user feedback loop signals into the evaluation component, the final system accuracy can be further improved. Even with 50% label noise, the system achieves 71.33% accuracy. The active learning system can achieve the same accuracy only after adding extra 800K manually labeled data. It's also worth noting that with the same noisy blurred label dataset, the supervised learning approach has much worse performance. Its classifier accuracy significantly drops to 57.8% with 100K golden label and 1.3M blurred labels at 20% noise level.

5.2 E-commerce Product Categorization Dataset Experiments

The proposed method is derived to tackle large scale text classification problems that occur in the e-Commerce industry, where the challenge is that we *significantly* lacked high-quality labeled data for these problems. For example, the e-commerce product categorization dataset contains product titles and 600 different categories for the product titles. This dataset contains four different parts: the product category description data for 600 categories, a 6K observation manually labeled initial training dataset L, a 28K observation manually labeled blind test set T, and a 3.5 million observation unlabeled dataset U that included rich user feedback session data F. The main task here is to predict the product category as soon as the online user enters the product title. For example, the user might enter a product title, such as green coach bag to describe a product. The system should classify this input title into the most relevant product category, such as "women's purse & bag". The 3.5 million unlabeled user behavior dataset contains a seller chosen category and a category suggested by a machine learning model. We consider these data to be unlabeled since the seller chosen category has a greater than 30% error rate according to our evaluations. The reason for this high error rate is due to the fact that the users are not familiar with the category tree or they just intentionally select the wrong category to increase the chance of selling their product. Note that for the main-task system that runs online, only the product title information is available to main-task model.

5.2.1 Results

With the initial 6K labeled dataset L, the 3.5M unlabeled dataset U and the 3.5M feedback session dataset F, we compare our proposed EMAEC approach with the auxiliary evaluation component to a weak supervised learning baseline and co-training baseline as described below. Similar to the previous set of experiments, once the labeled training corpus for the main model is derived, we use the shallow neural network classifier described in Joulin et al. (2016) to train $Main$.

1. **Supervised Learning with Small Labeled Data:** We train a supervised baseline model with the 6K labeled dataset L. This is the weak baseline model. Any proposed method that leverages unlabeled data U and session data F should outperform this number.

2. **Supervised Learning with Noisy Data:** We treat the 3.5M seller-chosen category as the correct labeled data from F, and then mix it with the 6K labeled dataset L to train a supervised

Model	Error Reduction Rate [%]
Supervised Learning with 6K Label Data	0.00
Supervised Learning with Noisy Data	12.30
Co-Training	15.20
EMAEC	19.23

Table 2: EMAEC gain in error reduction rate [%] compared to the co-training baseline on the e-commerce dataset

model. Total error reduction rate by adding seller-chosen labels is 12.3%

3. **Co-Training:** Use L to build two initial models and use U data in a co-training setup to enhance the initial models. Different feature sets from F are used to train two different models. After approximately 30 iterations, the system will converge to best performance. Total error reduction rate for co-training is 15.2%.

4. **EMAEC with Enriched Data:** Build the initial classifier $Main$ using L and F. Apply Algorithm 1 and Algorithm 2 to iteratively train the $Main$ and $Eval$ models. After approximately 20 iterations, the main task classifier $Main$ converges to its best performance. Total error reduction for our approach is 19.23%.

5.2.2 Discussions

The experiment results on the e-commerce product categorization dataset are summarized in table 2. The results demonstrate that our proposed approach with the auxiliary evaluation component outperforms the co-training approach substantially. The classification error rate is reduced by 5%. This improvement is well aligned with the results on the public Yahoo! Answers dataset.

6 Conclusions

In this paper, we proposed a semi-supervised learning approach to tackle the challenge of lacking high-quality labeled data. The experimental results in text classification tasks with both open source Yahoo! Answer data and our e-commerce data show the effectiveness of the proposed approach. This general dual player machine learning framework can also be applied to other machine learning tasks, such as search ranking, speech recognition, machine translation, etc.

The proposed method comes with advantages and disadvantages over existing semi-supervised learning approaches. The advantages have been demonstrated in text classification tasks in that it can automatically extract fairly high-quality predicted labeled data from massive unlabeled data. Thus, it can further improve prediction accuracy by adding those automatically enriched labeled data into the original training corpus.

On the other side, a potential drawback could be that its effectiveness may be limited by the prediction performance of the auxiliary evaluation model. If the auxiliary evaluation model is not able to generate many labeled samples with low false positive rate, the automatically enriched labeled data might not be well distributed to reflect the real problems underlying data distribution. To overcome this, we must rely on vast amounts of real-world unlabeled data.

At last, we know that the GAN based approach Goodfellow et al. (2014); Yu et al. (2017); and Kusner and Hernández-Lobato (2016) can automatically generate infinite amounts of fake data. Combining the advantages of the GAN framework and the proposed approach is a very interesting research direction for us in the future.

References

Alina Beygelzimer, Sanjoy Dasgupta, and John Langford. 2009. Importance weighted active learning. In *Proceedings of the 26th annual international conference on machine learning*, pages 49–56. ACM.

Avrim Blum and Tom Mitchell. 1998. Combining labeled and unlabeled data with co-training. In *Proceedings of the eleventh annual conference on Computational learning theory*, pages 92–100. ACM.

Minmin Chen, Kilian Q Weinberger, and John Blitzer. 2011. Co-training for domain adaptation. In *Advances in neural information processing systems*, pages 2456–2464.

Tianqi Chen and Carlos Guestrin. 2016. Xgboost: A scalable tree boosting system. In *Proceedings of the 22Nd ACM SIGKDD International Conference on Knowledge Discovery and Data Mining*, pages 785–794. ACM.

David A Cohn, Zoubin Ghahramani, and Michael I Jordan. 1996. Active learning with statistical models. *NIPS*.

A. P. Dempster, N. M. Laird, and D. B. Rubin. 1977. Maximum likelihood from incomplete data via the em algorithm. *JOURNAL OF THE ROYAL STATISTICAL SOCIETY, SERIES B*, 39(1):1–38.

I. Goodfellow, J. Pouget-Abadie, M. Mirza, B. Xu, D. Warde-Farley, S. Ozair, A. Courville, and Y. Bengio. 2014. Generative adversarial nets. *Advances in neural information processing systems*, pages 2672–2680.

Kenneth Heafield. 2011. KenLM: faster and smaller language model queries. In *Proceedings of the EMNLP 2011 Sixth Workshop on Statistical Machine Translation*, pages 187–197, Edinburgh, Scotland, United Kingdom.

A. Joulin, E. Grave, P. Bojanowski, and T. Mikolov. 2016. Bag of tricks for efficient text classification. *arXiv:1607.01759*.

Matt J Kusner and José Miguel Hernández-Lobato. 2016. Gans for sequences of discrete elements with the gumbel-softmax distribution. *arXiv preprint arXiv:1611.04051*.

Kamal Nigam, Andrew McCallum, Sebastian Thrun, Tom Mitchell, et al. 1998. Learning to classify text from labeled and unlabeled documents. *AAAI/IAAI*, 792.

Isaac Triguero, Salvador Garca, and Francisco Herrera. 2015. Self-labeled techniques for semi-supervised learning: Taxonomy, software and empirical study. *Knowledge and Information Systems*.

Isaac Triguero, José A Sáez, Julián Luengo, Salvador García, and Francisco Herrera. 2014. On the characterization of noise filters for self-training semi-supervised in nearest neighbor classification. *Neurocomputing*, 132:30–41.

Karl Weiss, Taghi M Khoshgoftaar, and DingDing Wang. 2016. A survey of transfer learning. *Journal of Big Data*, 3(1):1–40.

Songbai Yan, Kamalika Chaudhuri, and Tara Javidi. 2016. Active learning from imperfect labelers. In *Advances in Neural Information Processing Systems*, pages 2128–2136.

David Yarowsky. 1995. Unsupervised word sense disambiguation rivaling supervised methods. In *Proceedings of the 33rd annual meeting on Association for Computational Linguistics*, pages 189–196. Association for Computational Linguistics.

Lantao Yu, Weinan Zhang, Jun Wang, and Yong Yu. 2017. Seqgan: Sequence generative adversarial nets with policy gradient. In *AAAI*, pages 2852–2858.

Chicheng Zhang and Kamalika Chaudhuri. 2015. Active learning from weak and strong labelers. In *Advances in Neural Information Processing Systems*, pages 703–711.

Xiang Zhang, Junbo Zhao, and Yann LeCun. 2015. Character-level convolutional networks for text classification. *NIPS*.

Xiaojin Zhu and Andrew B Goldberg. 2009. Introduction to semi-supervised learning. *Synthesis lectures on artificial intelligence and machine learning*, 3(1):1–130.

Low-rank passthrough neural networks

Antonio Valerio Miceli Barone *

School of Informatics, The University of Edinburgh

`amiceli@inf.ed.ac.uk`

Abstract

Various common deep learning architectures, such as LSTMs, GRUs, Resnets and Highway Networks, employ state passthrough connections that support training with high feed-forward depth or recurrence over many time steps. These "Passthrough Networks" architectures also enable the decoupling of the network state size from the number of parameters of the network, a possibility has been studied by Sak et al. (2014) with their low-rank parametrization of the LSTM. In this work we extend this line of research, proposing effective, low-rank and low-rank plus diagonal matrix parametrizations for Passthrough Networks which exploit this decoupling property, reducing the data complexity and memory requirements of the network while preserving its memory capacity. This is particularly beneficial in low-resource settings as it supports expressive models with a compact parametrization less susceptible to overfitting. We present competitive experimental results on several tasks, including language modeling and a near state of the art result on sequential randomly-permuted MNIST classification, a hard task on natural data.

1 Overview

Deep neural networks can perform non-trivial computations by the repeated the application of parametric non-linear transformation layers to vectorial data. This staging of many computation steps can be done over a time dimension for tasks involving sequential inputs or outputs of varying length, yielding a *recurrent neural network*, or over an intrinsic circuit depth dimension, yielding a *deep feed-forward neural network*, or both. Training these deep models is complicated by the *exploding* and *vanishing* gradient problems (Hochreiter, 1991; Bengio et al., 1994).

Various network architectures have been proposed to ameliorate the vanishing gradient problem in the recurrent setting, such as the LSTM (Hochreiter and Schmidhuber, 1997; Graves and Schmidhuber, 2005), the GRU (Cho et al., 2014), the RHN (Zilly et al., 2016), etc. Similar methods have also been applied in the feed-forward setting with architectures such as Highway Networks (Srivastava et al., 2015), Deep Residual Networks (He et al., 2015), and so on. All these architectures are based on a single structural principle which, in this work, we will refer to as the *state passthrough*. We will thus refer to these architectures as *Passthrough Networks*.

In many settings, especially low-resource natural language processing tasks, the main difficulty in training neural networks is the trade-off between the network representation power and its training data complexity, which is related to the number of trainable parameters.

On one hand, the number of parameters can be thought as the number of tunable "knobs" that need to be set to represent a function, on the other hand, it also constrains the size of the partial results that are propagated inside the network. In typical fully connected networks, a layer acting on a n-dimensional state vector has $O(n^2)$ parameters stored in one or more matrices, but there can be many functions of practical interest that are simple enough to be represented by a relatively small number of bits while still requiring some sizable amount of memory in order to be computed. Therefore, representing these functions on

---

Work partially done while affiliated with University of Pisa.

77

Proceedings of the Workshop on Deep Learning Approaches for Low-Resource NLP, pages 77–86
Melbourne, Australia July 19, 2018. ©2018 Association for Computational Linguistics

a fully connected neural network can be wasteful in terms of number of parameters. The full parameterization implies that, at each step, all the information in each state component can affect all the information in any state component at the next step. Classical physical systems, however, consist of spatially separated parts with primarily local interactions, long-distance interactions are possible but they tend to be limited by propagation delays, bandwidth and noise. Therefore it may be beneficial to bias our model class towards models that tend to adhere to these physical constraints by using a parametrization which reduces the number of parameters required to represent them. This can be accomplished by imposing some constraints on the $n \times n$ matrices that parametrize the state transitions. One way of doing this is to impose a convolutional structure on these matrices (LeCun et al., 2004; Krizhevsky et al., 2012), which corresponds to strict locality and periodicity constraints as in a cellular automaton. These constraints work well in certain domains such as vision, but may be overly restrictive in other domains.

The state passthrough allows for a systematic decoupling of the network state size from the number of parameters: since by default the state vector passes mostly unaltered through the layers, each layer can be made simple enough to be described only by a small number of parameters without affecting the overall memory capacity of the network, effectively spreading the computation over the depth or time dimension of the network, but without making the network "thin". This has been exploited by some convolutional passthrough architectures (Srivastava et al., 2015; He et al., 2015; Kaiser and Sutskever, 2015), or architectures with addressable read-write memory (Graves et al., 2014; Danihelka et al., 2016).

In this work we propose simple but effective low-dimensional parametrizations that exploit this decoupling based on low-rank or low-rank plus diagonal matrix decompositions. Our approach extends the LSTM architecture with a single projection layer proposed by Sak et al. (2014) which has been applied to speech recognition, natural language modeling (Józefowicz et al., 2016), video analysis (Sun et al., 2015), etc. We provide experimental evaluation of our approach on GRU and LSTM architectures on various machine learning tasks, including a near state of the art result for the hard task of sequential randomly-permuted

MNIST image recognition (Le et al., 2015).

2 Model

2.1 Passthrough networks

A (fixed-width) neural network can be described as a dynamical system with a n-dimensional state vector $x(t) \in \mathcal{R}^n$ that transforms an input u into an output y over multiple time steps T.

Passthrough networks can be defined as networks where the state evolves according to a transition function f which has a special form such that, at each step t the state vector $x(t)$ is propagated to the next step modified only by some (nearly) linear, element-wise transformation.

We define a network to have a *state passthrough* on x if x evolves as

$$x(t) = \pi(t) \odot \tau(t) + x(t-1) \odot \gamma(t) \qquad (1)$$

where π is the *next state proposal*, τ is the *state transform*, γ is the *state carry* and $\odot$ denotes element-wise vector multiplication.

Additional non-passthrough state vectors may be also present[1].

As concrete example, we can describe the fully connected Gated Recurrent Unit (GRU) by Cho et al. (2014) as

$$\omega(t) = \sigma(\theta^{W_\omega} u(t) + \theta^{U_\omega} x(t-1))$$
$$\gamma(t) = \sigma(\theta^{W_\gamma} u(t) + \theta^{U_\gamma} x(t-1))$$
$$\tau(t) = 1^{\otimes n} - \gamma(t)$$
$$\pi(t) = g(\theta^{W_\pi} u(t) + \theta^{(U_\pi)} (x(t-1) \odot \omega(t)))$$
$$(2)$$

where g is the hyperbolic tangent, σ is the logistic sigmoid, $\theta^{W_\omega}, \theta^{W_\gamma}, \theta^{W_\pi} \in \mathcal{R}^{n \times m}$ are input parameter matrices and $\theta^{U_\omega}, \theta^{U_\gamma}, \theta^{U_\pi} \in \mathcal{R}^{n \times n}$ are the recurrent parameter matrices (bias vectors θ^b- not shown). $\omega(t)$ is the *reset gate* which is specific to the GRU architecture.

2.2 Low-rank passthrough networks

We can impose a low-rank constraint on the state transition matrices by rewriting each of them as the product of two matrices, where the inner dimension d is a model hyperparameter.

In the case of the GRU of eq. 2 we can redefine

---

[1]For instance the LSTM has a passthrough "cell" state and a non-passthrough "hidden" state.

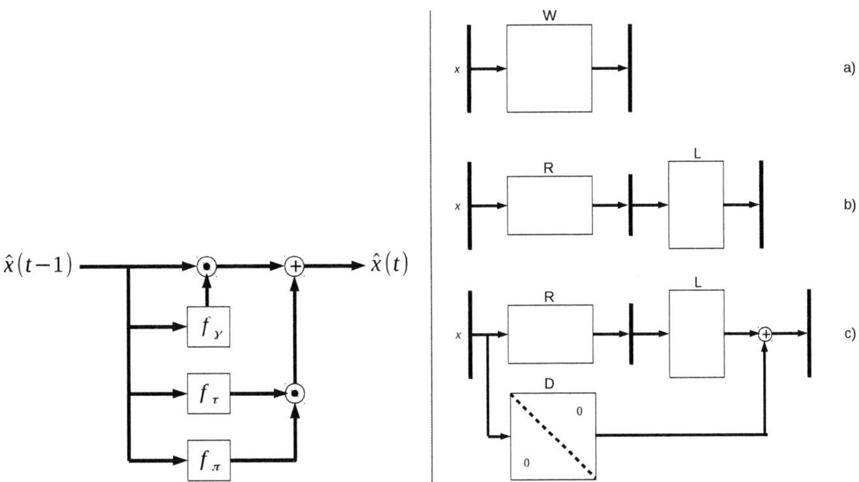

Figure 1: Left: Generic state passthrough hidden layer, optional per-timestep input $u(t)$ is not shown. Right: a) Full matrix parametrization. b) Low-rank parametrization. c) Low-rank plus diagonal parametrization.

the recurrent parameter matrices as

$$\theta^{(U_\omega)} = \theta^{(L_\omega)} \cdot \theta^{(R_\omega)}$$
$$\theta^{(U_\gamma)} = \theta^{(L_\gamma)} \cdot \theta^{(R_\gamma)} \qquad (3)$$
$$\theta^{(U_\pi)} = \theta^{(L_\pi)} \cdot \theta^{(R_\pi)}$$

where $\theta^{(L_-)} \in \mathcal{R}^{n \times d}$ and $\theta^{(R_-)}, \in \mathcal{R}^{d \times n}$. When $d < n/2$ this result in a reduction of the number of trainable parameters of the model.

Even when $n/2 \le d < n$, while the total number of parameter increases, the number of degrees of freedom of the model still decreases, because low-rank factorization are unique only up to arbitrary $d \times d$ invertible matrices, thus the number of independent degrees of freedom of a low-rank layer is $2nd - d^2$.

This low-rank constraint can be thought as a bandwidth constraint on the computation performed at each step: the R matrices first project the state into a smaller subspace, extracting the information needed for that specific step, then the L matrices project it back to the original state space, spreading the selected information to all the state components that need to be updated.

In this parametrization, which we denote as *untied low-rank*, we allow each parameter matrix to be parametrized independently by a pair of R and L matrices. This extends the approach of Sak et al. (2014) for the LSTM architecture, which we denote here as *tied low-rank*, where they instead force the R matrices to be the same for all the functions of the state transition.

A low-rank parametrization can be also applied to the input matrices of recurrent neural networks, in fact, the input embedding layer commonly used in NLP applications results in a tied low-rank parametrization of the input whenever the embedding size is lower than the RNN state size.

Low-rank passthrough architectures are universal in that they retain the same representation classes of their parent architectures. This equivalence can be realized in the worst case by exploiting a depth-rank tradeoff (e.g. either $O(n)$ rank and $O(T)$ depth or $O(1)$ rank and $O(nT)$ depth)[2].

2.3 Low-rank plus diagonal passthrough networks

As we show in the experimental section, on some tasks the low-rank constraint may prove to be excessively restrictive if the goal is to train a model with fewer parameters than one with arbitrary matrices. A simple extension is to add to each low-rank parameter matrix a diagonal parameter matrix, yielding a matrix that is full-rank but still parametrized in a low-dimensional space. For instance, for the GRU we modify eq. 3 to

$$\theta^{(U_\omega)} = \theta^{(L_\omega)} \cdot \theta^{(R_\omega)} + \theta^{(D_\omega)}$$
$$\theta^{(U_\gamma)} = \theta^{(L_\gamma)} \cdot \theta^{(R_\gamma)} + \theta^{(D_\gamma)} \qquad (4)$$
$$\theta^{(U_\pi)} = \theta^{(L_\pi)} \cdot \theta^{(R_\pi)} + \theta^{(D_\pi)}$$

---

[2]In the case of recurrent networks, depth is intended as the *recurrence depth* (Zilly et al., 2016).

where $\theta^{(D_-)}$ are trainable diagonal parameter matrices.

It may seem that adding diagonal parameter matrices is redundant in passthrough networks. After all, the state passthrough itself can be considered as a diagonal matrix applied to the state vector, which is then additively combined to the new proposed state computed by the f_π function. However, since the state passthrough completely skips over all non-linear activation functions, these formulations are not equivalent. In particular, the low-rank plus diagonal parametrization may help in recurrent neural networks which receive input at each time step, since it allows each component of the state vector to directly control how much input signal is inserted into it at each step. We demonstrate the effectiveness of this model for the sequence copy, sequential MNIST and language modeling tasks described in the experiments section.

3 Experiments

We applied the Low-rank GRU (LR-GRU) and Low-rank plus diagonal GRU (LRD-GRU) architectures to a subset of sequential benchmarks described in the Unitary Evolution Recurrent Neural Networks (uRNN) article by Arjovsky et al. (2015), specifically the memory task, the addition task and the sequential randomly permuted MNIST task. For the memory tasks, we also considered two different variants proposed by Danihelka et al. (2016) and Henaff et al. (2016) which are hard for the uRNN architecture. We chose to compare against the uRNN architecture because it set state of the art results in terms of both data complexity and accuracy and because it is an architecture with similar design objectives as low-rank passthrough architectures, namely a low-dimensional parametrization and the mitigation of the vanishing gradient problem, but it is based on quite different principles.

We also applied these architectures to a character-level language modeling task on the Penn Treebank corpus. For the language modeling task, we also experimented with Low-rank plus diagonal LSTMs.

3.1 Memory task

The input of an instance of this task is a sequence of $T = N + 20$ discrete symbols in a ten symbol alphabet $a_i : i \in 0, \ldots 9$, encoded as one-hot

vectors. The first 10 symbols in the sequence are "data" symbols i.i.d. sampled from $a_0, \ldots, a_7$, followed by $N - 1$ "blank" a_8 symbols, then a distinguished "run" symbol a_9, followed by 10 more "blank" a_8 symbols. The desired output sequence consists of $N + 10$ "blank" a_8 symbols followed by the 10 "data" symbols as they appeared in the input sequence. Therefore the model has to remember the 10 "data" symbol string over the temporal gap of size N, which is challenging for a recurrent neural network when N is large. In our experiment we set $N = 500$, which is the hardest setting explored in the uRNN work. The training set consists of $100,000$ training examples and $10,000$ validation/test examples. The architecture is a GRU with a dense $n \times 10$ output matrix followed a (biased) softmax. We train to minimize the cross-entropy loss.

We were able to solve this task using a GRU with full recurrent matrices with state size $n = 128$, learning rate 1×10^{-3}, mini-batch size 20, initial bias of the carry functions (the "update" gates) 4.0, however this model has many more parameters, nearly $50,000$ in the recurrent layer only, than the uRNN work which has about $6,500$, and it converges much more slowly than the uRNN. We were not able to achieve convergence with a pure low-rank model without exceeding the number of parameters of the fully connected model, but we achieved fast convergence with a LRD-GRU model with $d = 50$, with other hyperparameters set as above. This model has still more parameters ($39,168$ in the recurrent layer, $41,738$ total) than the uRNN model and converges more slowly but still reasonably fast, reaching test cross-entropy $< 1 \times 10^{-3}$ nats and almost perfect classification accuracy in less than $35,000$ updates.

In order to obtain a fair comparison, we also train a uRNN model with state size $n = 721$, resulting in approximately the same number of parameters as the LRD-GRU models. This model very quickly reaches perfect accuracy on the training set in less than $2,000$ updates, but overfits w.r.t. the test set.

We also consider two variants of this task which are difficult for the uRNN model. For both these tasks we used the same settings as above except that the task size parameter is set at $N = 100$ for consistency with the works that introduced these variants. In the variant of Danihelka et al. (2016), the length of the sequence to be remembered is

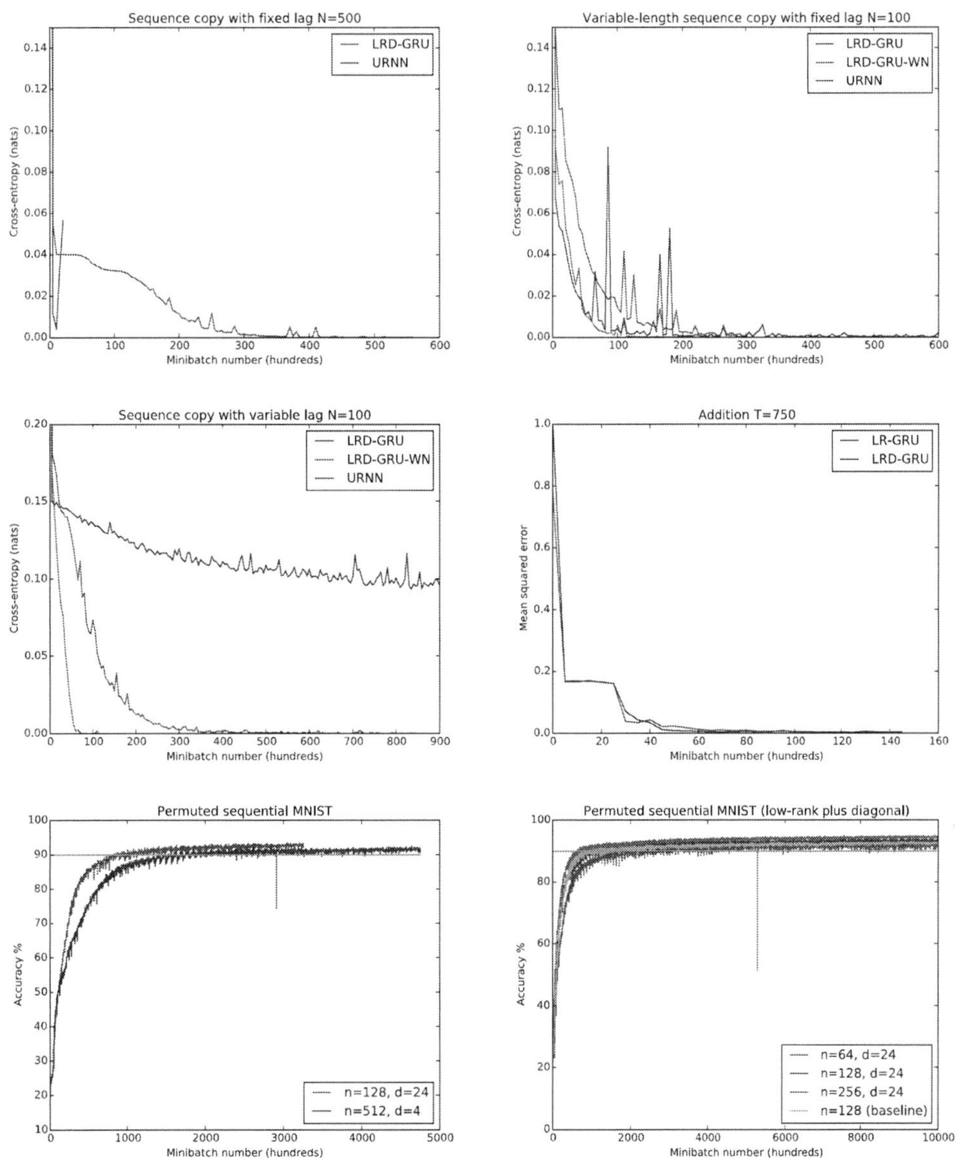

Figure 2: Top row and middle left: LRD-GRU and uRNN on the sequence copy tasks, cross-entropy on validation set. Middle right: LR-GRU and LRD-GRU on the addition task, mean squared error on validation set. Bottom row: LR-GRU (left) and LRD-GRU (right) on the permuted sequential MNIST task, accuracy on validation set, horizontal line indicates 90% accuracy.

randomly sampled between 1 and 10 for each sequence. They manage to achieve fast convergence with their Associative LSTM architecture with $65, 505$ parameters, and slower convergence with standard LSTM models. Our LRD-GRU architecture, which has less parameters than their Associative LSTM, performs comparably or better, reaching test cross-entropy $< 1 \times 10^{-3}$ nats and almost perfect classification accuracy in less than $30, 000$ updates. In the variant of Henaff et al. (2016), the length of the sequence to be remembered is fixed at 10 but the model is expected to copy it after a variable number of time steps randomly chosen, for each sequence, between 1 and $N = 100$. The authors achieve slow convergence with a standard LSTM model, while our LRD-GRU architecture achieves fast convergence, reaching test cross-entropy $< 1 \times 10^{-3}$ nats and almost perfect classification accuracy in less than $38, 000$ updates, and perfect test accuracy in $87, 000$ updates.

We further train uRNN models with state size $n = 721$ on these variants of the memory task. We found that the uRNN learns faster than the LRD-GRU on the variable length, fixed lag task (Danihelka et al., 2016) but fails to converge within our training time limit on the fixed length, variable lag task (Henaff et al., 2016).

Training the LRD-GRU on these tasks incurs sometimes in numerical stability problems as discussed in sec. 3.5.1. In order to systemically address these issues, we also trained models with weight normalization (Salimans and Kingma, 2016) and weight row max-norm constraints. These models turned out to be more stable and in fact converge faster, performing on par with the uRNN on the variable length, fixed lag task.

Training curves are shown in figure 2 (top and middle left).

3.2 Addition task

For each instance of this task, the input sequence has length T and consists of two real-valued components, at each step the first component is independently sampled from the interval $[0, 1]$ with uniform probability, the second component is equal to zero everywhere except at two randomly chosen time step, one in each half of the sequence, where it is equal to one. The result is a single real value computed from the final state which we want to be equal to the sum of the two elements of the first component of the sequence at the positions

where the second component was set at one. In our experiment we set $T = 750$.

The training set consists of $100, 000$ training examples and $10, 000$ validation/test examples. We use a LR-GRU and a LRD-GRU with $2 \times n$ input matrix, $n \times 1$ output matrix and (biased) identity output activation. We train to minimize the mean squared error loss. We use state size $n = 128$, maximum rank $d = 24$. This results in approximately $6, 140$ parameters in the recurrent hidden layer. Learning rate was set at 1×10^{-3}, mini-batch size 20, initial bias of the carry functions (the "update" gates) was set to 4.

We trained on $14, 500$ mini-batches, obtaining a mean squared error on the test set of 0.003 for both parametrizations, which is a better result than the one reported in the uRNN article, in terms of training time and final accuracy. The training curves are shown in figure 2 (middle right).

3.3 Sequential MNIST task

This task consists of handwritten digit classification on the MNIST dataset with the caveat that the input is presented to the model one pixel value at time, over $T = 784$ time steps. To further increase the difficulty of the task, the inputs are reordered according to a random permutation (fixed for all the task instances).

We use LR-GRUs and a LRD-GRUs with $1 \times n$ input matrix, $n \times 10$ output matrix and (biased) softmax output activation. Learning rate was set at 5×10^{-4}, mini-batch size 20, initial bias of the carry functions (the "update" gates) was set to 5.

Results are presented in table 1 and training curves are shown in figure 2 (bottom row). All these models except the one with the most extreme bottleneck ($n = 512, d = 4$) exceed the reported uRNN test accuracy of 91.4%, although they converge more slowly (hundred of thousands updates vs. tens of thousands of the uRNN). Also note that the LRD-GRU is more accurate than the full-rank GRU with the same state size, while the LR-GRU is slightly less accurate (in terms of test accuracy), indicating the utility of the diagonal component of the parametrization for this task.

These are on par with more complex architectures with time-skip connections (Zhang et al., 2016) (reported test set accuracy 94.0%). To our knowledge, at the time of this writing, the best result on this task is the LSTM with recurrent batch normalization by Cooijmans et al. (2016)

Table 1: Sequential permuted MNIST results

Architecture	state size	max rank	params	val. accuracy	test accuracy
Baseline GRU	128	-	51.0 k	93.0%	92.8%
LR-GRU	128	24	20.2 k	93.4%	91.8%
LR-GRU	512	4	19.5 k	92.5%	91.3%
LRD-GRU	64	24	10.3 k	93.1%	91.9%
LRD-GRU	128	24	20.6 k	94.1%	93.5%
LRD-GRU	256	24	41.2 k	**95.1%**	**94.7%**

(reported test set accuracy 95.2%). The architectural innovations of these works are orthogonal to our own and in principle they can be combined to it.

3.4 Character-level language modeling task

This standard benchmark task consist of predicting the probability of the next character in a sentence after having observed the previous charters. Following Zaremba et al. (2014), we use the Penn Treebank English corpus, with standard training, validation and test splits. As a baseline we use a single layer GRU either with no regularization or regularized with Bayesian recurrent dropout (Gal, 2015).

In our experiments we primarily consider the LRD-GRU, both with tied and untied projection matrices. We set the state size and maximum rank to either reduce the total number of parameters compared to the baselines or to keep the number of parameters approximately the same while increasing the memory capacity. We also compare with the LR-GRU. Results are shown in table 2.

Our LRD-GRU reduces the model per-character perplexity (the base-2 exponential of the bits-per-character entropy). Both the tied and untied versions perform equally when the state size is the same, but the tied version performs better when the number of parameters is kept the same, presumably due to the increased memory capacity of the state vector. Our best model has an extreme bottleneck, over a hundred of times smaller than the state size, while the word-level language models trained by Józefowicz et al. (2016) use bottlenecks of four to eight times smaller than the state size. This difference is likely due to our usage of the "plus diagonal" parametrization, in fact, the plain LR-GRU with such an extreme bottleneck fails to even approach the baselines.

In terms of absolute perplexity, our results are worse than published ones (e.g. Graves (2013)), although they may not be directly comparable since published results generally use different training and evaluation schemes, such as preserving the network state between different sentences.

We ran additional experiments using LSTM architectures, similar to Graves (2013), although we still could not obtain the same baseline performance even using the Adam optimizer (using SGD+momentum yields even worse results). In fact, we obtained approximately the same perplexity as our baseline GRU model with the same state size.

We applied the Low-rank plus diagonal parametrizations to our LSTM architecture maintaining the same number of parameters as the baseline. We obtained notable perplexity improvements over the baseline.

3.5 Experimental details

3.5.1 Low-rank GRUs

In our experiments (except language modeling) we optimized using RMSProp (Tieleman and Hinton, 2012) with gradient component clipping at 1. Code is available online [3]. Our code is based on the published uRNN code[4] (specifically, on the LSTM implementation) by the original authors for the sake of a fair comparison. In order to achieve convergence on the memory task however, we had to slightly modify the optimization procedure, specifically we changed gradient component clipping with gradient norm clipping (with NaN detection and recovery), and we added a small $\epsilon = 1 \times 10^{-8}$ term in the parameter update formula. No modifications of the original optimizer implementation were required for the other tasks.

In order to address the numerical instability issues in the memory tasks, we also consider a variant of our LRD-GRU where apply weight nor-

---

[3] https://github.com/Avmb/lowrank-gru
[4] https://github.com/amarshah/complex_RNN

Table 2: Character-level language modeling results

Architecture	dropout	tied	state size	max rank	params	test char perplexity
Baseline GRU	No	-	1000	-	3.11 M	2.96
Baseline GRU	Yes	-	1000	-	3.11 M	2.92
Baseline GRU	Yes	-	3298	-	33.0 M	2.77
Baseline LSTM	Yes	-	1000	-	4.25 M	2.92
LRD-GRU	No	No	1000	64	0.49 M	2.92
LRD-GRU	No	No	3298	128	2.89 M	2.95
LRD-GRU	Yes	No	3298	128	2.89 M	2.86
LRD-GRU	Yes	No	5459	64	2.69 M	2.82
LRD-GRU	Yes	Yes	5459	64	1.99 M	2.81
LRD-GRU	No	Yes	1000	64	0.46 M	2.90
LRD-GRU	Yes	Yes	4480	128	2.78 M	2.86
LRD-GRU	Yes	Yes	6985	64	2.54 M	**2.76**
LR-GRU	Yes	Yes	6985	64	2.54 M	9.88
LRD-LSTM	Yes	No	1740	300	4.25 M	2.86

malization as described by Salimans and Kingma (2016) to all the parameter matrices except the output one and the diagonal matrices. All these matrices have trainable scale parameters, except for the projection (R) matrices. We further apply a hard constraint on the matrices row norms by clipping them at 10 after each update. We disable NaN detection and recovery during training. The rationale behind this approach, in addition to the general benefits of normalization, is that the low-rank parametrization potentially introduces stability issues because the model is invariant to the simultaneous multiplication of a row of an R-matrix by a scalar s and the division of the corresponding column of the L-matrix by s, which in principle allows the parameters of either matrix to grow very large in magnitude, eventually resulting in overflows or other pathological behavior. The weight row max-norm constraint can counter this problem. But the constraint alone could make the optimization problem harder by restricting and distorting the parameter space. Fortunately we can counter this by weight normalization which makes the model invariant to the row-norms of the parameter matrices.

In the language modeling experiment, the character vocabulary size is 51, we use no character embeddings. Training is performed with Adam with learning rate 1×10^{-3}. Bayesian recurrent dropout was adapted from the original LSTM architecture of Gal (2015) to the GRU architecture as in Sennrich et al. (2016).

Our implementation is based on the "dl4mt" tutorial[5] and the Nematus neural machine translation system [6]. The code is available online [7].

3.5.2 Low-rank LSTMs

For our LSTM experiments, we modified the implementation of LSTM language model with Bayesian recurrent dropout by Gal (2015)[8]. In order to match the setup of Graves (2013) more closely, we used a vocabulary size of 49, no embedding layer and one LSTM layer. We the Adam optimizer with learning rate 2×10^{-4}. The low-rank plus diagonal parametrization is applied on the recurrence matrices as in the GRU models. The code is available online[9].

4 Conclusions

We proposed low-dimensional parametrizations for passthrough neural networks based on low-rank or low-rank plus diagonal decompositions of the $n \times n$ matrices that occur in the hidden layers. We experimentally compared our models with state of the art models, obtaining competitive results including a near state of the art for the randomly-permuted sequential MNIST task,

[5]https://github.com/nyu-dl/dl4mt-tutorial
[6]https://github.com/EdinburghNLP/nematus
[7]https://github.com/Avmb/dl4mt-lm/tree/master/lm
[8]https://github.com/yaringal/BayesianRNN
[9] https://github.com/Avmb/lowrank-lstm

and improvements over the baselines on a language modeling task. We showed that the LRD parametrization outperforms the LR parametrization in almost all task and never underpeforms it, which highlight as the main contribution of this work. Therefore recommend to always include a diagonal parameter matrix whenever a low-rank parametrization is used. We also presented a weight row-norm constraint trick to improve optimization stability for these kind of architectures with multiplicative symmetries.

References

Martin Arjovsky, Amar Shah, and Yoshua Bengio. 2015. Unitary evolution recurrent neural networks. *CoRR*, abs/1511.06464.

Yoshua Bengio, Patrice Simard, and Paolo Frasconi. 1994. Learning long-term dependencies with gradient descent is difficult. *Neural Networks, IEEE Transactions on*, 5(2):157–166.

Kyunghyun Cho, Bart van Merrienboer, Caglar Gulcehre, Fethi Bougares, Holger Schwenk, and Yoshua Bengio. 2014. Learning phrase representations using rnn encoder-decoder for statistical machine translation. *arXiv preprint arXiv:1406.1078*.

T. Cooijmans, N. Ballas, C. Laurent, Ç. Gülçehre, and A. Courville. 2016. Recurrent Batch Normalization. *ArXiv e-prints*.

I. Danihelka, G. Wayne, B. Uria, N. Kalchbrenner, and A. Graves. 2016. Associative Long Short-Term Memory. *ArXiv e-prints*.

Yarin Gal. 2015. A theoretically grounded application of dropout in recurrent neural networks. *arXiv preprint arXiv:1512.05287*.

Alex Graves. 2013. Generating sequences with recurrent neural networks. *arXiv preprint arXiv:1308.0850*.

Alex Graves and Jürgen Schmidhuber. 2005. Framewise phoneme classification with bidirectional lstm and other neural network architectures. *Neural Networks*, 18(5):602–610.

Alex Graves, Greg Wayne, and Ivo Danihelka. 2014. Neural turing machines. *arXiv preprint arXiv:1410.5401*.

Kaiming He, Xiangyu Zhang, Shaoqing Ren, and Jian Sun. 2015. Deep residual learning for image recognition. *arXiv preprint arXiv:1512.03385*.

M. Henaff, A. Szlam, and Y. LeCun. 2016. Orthogonal RNNs and Long-Memory Tasks. *ArXiv e-prints*.

Sepp Hochreiter. 1991. Untersuchungen zu dynamischen neuronalen netzen. *Diploma, Technische Universität München*.

Sepp Hochreiter and Jürgen Schmidhuber. 1997. Long short-term memory. *Neural computation*, 9(8):1735–1780.

Rafal Józefowicz, Oriol Vinyals, Mike Schuster, Noam Shazeer, and Yonghui Wu. 2016. Exploring the limits of language modeling. *arXiv preprint arXiv:1602.02410*.

Lukasz Kaiser and Ilya Sutskever. 2015. Neural gpus learn algorithms. *CoRR*, abs/1511.08228.

Alex Krizhevsky, Ilya Sutskever, and Geoffrey E Hinton. 2012. Imagenet classification with deep convolutional neural networks. In *Advances in neural information processing systems*, pages 1097–1105.

Quoc V Le, Navdeep Jaitly, and Geoffrey E Hinton. 2015. A simple way to initialize recurrent networks of rectified linear units. *arXiv preprint arXiv:1504.00941*.

Yann LeCun, Fu Jie Huang, and Leon Bottou. 2004. Learning methods for generic object recognition with invariance to pose and lighting. In *Computer Vision and Pattern Recognition, 2004. CVPR 2004. Proceedings of the 2004 IEEE Computer Society Conference on*, volume 2, pages II–97. IEEE.

Hasim Sak, Andrew W Senior, and Françoise Beaufays. 2014. Long short-term memory recurrent neural network architectures for large scale acoustic modeling. In *INTERSPEECH*, pages 338–342.

Tim Salimans and Diederik P Kingma. 2016. Weight normalization: A simple reparameterization to accelerate training of deep neural networks. *arXiv preprint arXiv:1602.07868*.

Rico Sennrich, Barry Haddow, and Alexandra Birch. 2016. Edinburgh neural machine translation systems for wmt 16. *arXiv preprint arXiv:1606.02891*.

Rupesh Kumar Srivastava, Klaus Greff, and Jürgen Schmidhuber. 2015. Highway networks. *arXiv preprint arXiv:1505.00387*.

Chen Sun, Sanketh Shetty, Rahul Sukthankar, and Ram Nevatia. 2015. Temporal localization of fine-grained actions in videos by domain transfer from web images. In *Proceedings of the 23rd Annual ACM Conference on Multimedia Conference*, pages 371–380. ACM.

Tijmen Tieleman and Geoffrey Hinton. 2012. Lecture 6.5 - rmsprop,.

Wojciech Zaremba, Ilya Sutskever, and Oriol Vinyals. 2014. Recurrent neural network regularization. *arXiv preprint arXiv:1409.2329*.

Saizheng Zhang, Yuhuai Wu, Tong Che, Zhouhan Lin, Roland Memisevic, Ruslan Salakhutdinov, and Yoshua Bengio. 2016. Architectural complexity measures of recurrent neural networks. *arXiv preprint arXiv:1602.08210*.

Julian Georg Zilly, Rupesh Kumar Srivastava, Jan Koutník, and Jürgen Schmidhuber. 2016. Recurrent highway networks. *arXiv preprint arXiv:1607.03474*.

Author Index

Association for Computational Linguistics
209 N. Eighth Street
Stroudsburg, Pennsylvania 18360

ISBN 978-1-5108-6721-5